financial peace

for the next generation

Dave Ramsey

The Lampo Group, Inc.
1749 Mallory Lane - Suite 100
Brentwood, TN 37027

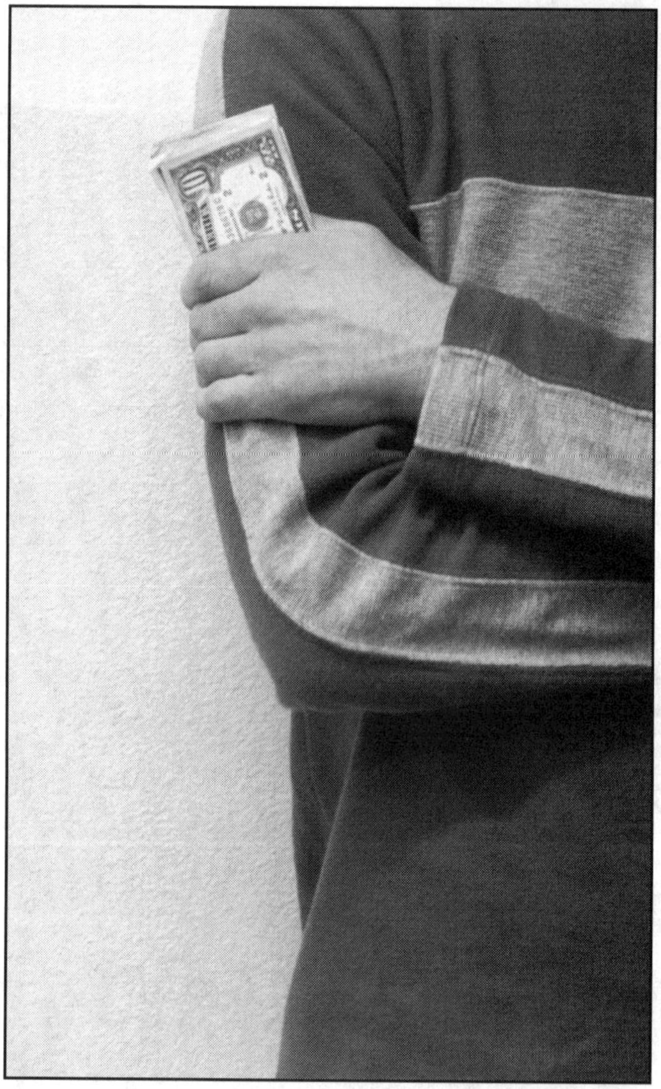

Acknowledgements

Workbook Adaptation by
Greg Carson

Project & Editorial Director
Mike Kennedy

Editorial Team
Cyndi Austin
Lisa Barber
Tony Bartoli
Tony Bradshaw
Leslie Bransford
Sheila Carson
Doug Finch
Kim Kennedy
Maria Riebe
Matt Woodburn
Sarah Wray

Editorial Updates
Amber Frey, Maria Riebe

Cover Design, Design Implementation and Page Production
Disciple Design

Corresponding Video Editing by
Zap Digital Media

Requests for permission to make copies of any part of the work should be mailed to:

Permissions - Youth Resources Department
The Lampo Group, Inc.
1749 Mallory Lane - Suite 100
Brentwood, TN 37027

Printed in the United States of America

ISBN 0-9720044-0-8

A Note To The Reader
This publication is designed to provide accurate and authoritative information with regard to the subject matter covered. It is sold with the understanding that the publisher is not engaged in rendering financial, accounting, or other professional advice. If financial advice or other expert professional assistance is required, the services of a competent professional person should be sought.

The Lampo Group would like to thank the following educators for their assistance with this project. We commend them for their commitment to excellence in empowering young adults through their journey to financial peace.

Workbook Adaptation By Greg Carson

Greg Carson is a graduate of Austin Peay State University and currently teaches Biology and Economics at Father Ryan High School in Nashville, Tennessee. He has taught the Financial Peace curriculum at Father Ryan since 1997. He and his wife Sheila live in the Nashville area with their two children, Sarah Beth and Bret.

Greg would like to thank the faculty, staff, students and administration of Father Ryan High School, Jack Langton, Therese Williams, Father Joe McMahon, John Spore, C. A. Williams, and Eddie Krenson for their support and promotion of the Financial Peace Curriculum.

Reviewers

Mike Brown
Math Teacher
Donelson Christian Academy
Nashville, TN

Tara Brown
Banking Economics Teacher
Antioch High School
Antioch, TN

Paul Compton
Principal
Brentwood Academy
Brentwood, TN

Marie Guilliams
Consumer Economics
Home School Leader
Tullahoma, TN

Connie Hansom
Admissions Director
Father Ryan High School
Nashville, TN

Keith Jowers
Financial Counselor & School Resource Officer
Baldwin Middle - Senior High School
Baldwin, FL

Len McKnatt
Economics Teacher
Battle Ground Academy
Franklin, TN

Steve Peden
Economics Teacher
Father Ryan High School
Nashville, TN

Kitty Robinson
Business Department Chair
Tolleson Union High School
Tolleson, AZ

Chris Shuff
Economics Teacher
Father Ryan High School
Nashville, TN

Cynthia Zeitz
Extension Agent
University of Tennesee
Agricultural Extension Service
Jackson County, TN

Special thanks to the students and faculty of Antioch High School - Antioch, TN and Father Ryan High School - Nashville, TN.

Table of Contents

unit 1

super savers

understanding investments

retirement and college planning

chapter 1

super savers

Objectives:

At the completion of this chapter, you should be able to:

- Explain the 3 basic reasons for saving money
- Define Compound Interest
- Explain the benefits of having a fully funded Emergency Fund
- Describe how a "Sinking Fund" approach works

Key Terms:

Amoral
Emergency Fund
Sinking Fund
Discipline
Compound Interest
PAC's

Pocket Change

- According to the *Wall Street Journal* nearly 70% of consumers live paycheck to paycheck.
- In the new millennium, the personal savings rate in America fell to –2.2%—the lowest in 60 years, according to the Department of Commerce.
- A Marist Institute poll published in the *USA Today* stated that 55% of Americans "always" or "sometimes" worry about their money.
- According to Automatic Data Processing, Inc., 20% of workers would not be able to make a mortgage, utility, or credit card payment if they missed a paycheck.
- *Money* magazine states that 75% of families will have a major negative financial event ($10,000) in any ten-year period.
- According to the July 11th, 2001 Oprah Winfrey Show, her own on-line survey revealed that 70% of respondents had NO savings.

The American Consumer is facing dire financial straits. After witnessing national trends and gathering information from personal observation over the past ten years, I am disturbed by the direction our management of money has taken.

Our nation's financial situation, with record budget deficits and bank failures, is deplorable. However, the nation's situation is only a reflection of our own personal inability to "Just Say No" to ourselves. Our failure to get control of financial matters in our personal lives will have to be rectified before we can demand accountability from elected officials. Our spoiled Congress is only a reflection of our spoiled selves. The good of our country is overlooked so our pet special-interest groups can be served, just like the good of the family is often overlooked so Dad or Mom can have that special trinket they must possess.

As a people we have forgotten how to delay pleasure. We are living in a society that microwaves everything. We must have it, and we must have it now! As Brian Tracy, a well-known motivational speaker, says, "We are being taught by everything around us to have dessert before dinner. Now we are paying for our lack of knowledge and discipline."

The statistics of financial failure show clearly that this decline is a fact. These statistics do not reveal cycles but rather, more alarmingly, show steady decline. These statistics do not show any attributable correlation with inflation, unemployment, recession, or any national trend except the rise in personal debt. Christian author Larry Burkett says that in 1929 only 2 percent of American homes had a mortgage and by 1962 only 2 percent didn't have mortgages.

We must not be misled into believing that these problems are faced only by large companies or deadbeats. On the contrary, these are typical American families with two kids, a dog, and dinner every night. I have met with these families and they are regular folks. Their situation just got out of control.

The *Consumer Reports Money Book* states that the typical American household has $38,000 in personal debt and total consumer debt has almost tripled just since 1980. A recent study in the *Wall Street Journal* states that 70 percent of the American public lives from paycheck to paycheck. Interestingly, a Marist Institute poll published right after that *Wall Street Journal* article stated that 55 percent of Americans "always" or "sometimes" worry about their money. If 70 percent are broke and only 55 percent are worried, I guess the other 15 percent are asleep.

The generation of people who set up housekeeping in the 1930's and 1940's was scarred by the Great Depression. Those folks would borrow very seldom, and they lived under their means. They would be shocked by the way most families live today.

The 1970's, 1980's, and 1990's have seen lending and borrowing at an all-time high in modern history. We want it all and we can borrow to get it all, before we can afford it all. Over the last forty years we have gradually become a nation of consumers, instead of the nation of producers we used to be.

Most Americans Are Not SAVERS!

Saving must become a ________________.

1.1 List 5 things that you consider to be priorities in your life, then tell why they are priorities.
1.
2.
3.
4.
5.

You must pay yourself ____________.
(If you were working for you, would you pay you? You had better!)

With your money you should Give, Save, and then pay __________.

If you do not make saving a priority, you will never do it.

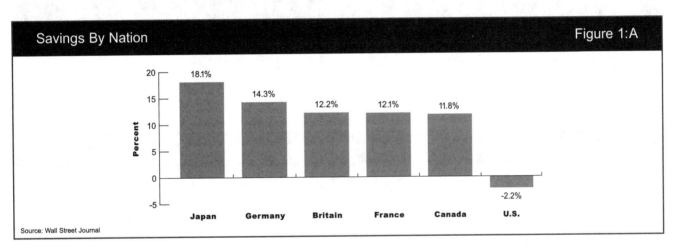

Savings By Nation — Figure 1:A

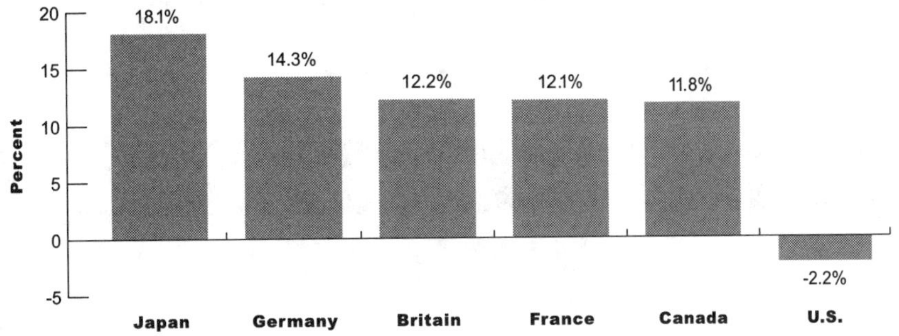

Source: Wall Street Journal

Any way you slice –2.2%, the translation is DEBT!

1.2 Are you currently saving money? Is it from a part-time job, your parents? Explain.

You have to be willing to make a sacrifice now or later! You can either:

- Spend everything now and have little or nothing at retirement…or
- Save some now, put off getting the "name brand stuff," and end up with several million dollars at retirement. You make the call.

Saving is about ____________ and ______________.

1.3 What brings you contentment in life? Is money attached to that?

1.4 Do you plan to rely on Social Security? Why or Why not?

Money is ____________.
(It is neither good nor bad.)

Author Larry Burkett says that the only difference between saving and hoarding is ______________.

1.5 Give an example of how money is used in a positive way…and an example of how it is used in a negative way.

1.6 Would you say that debt is a negative use of money? Why or why not?

You should save for 3 things: ________________

____

____

You have got to start saving right ________!

Compound Interest Is Powerful!

Take $1,000 and earn 10% on it. Your interest at the end of the year is $100. Add that to the $1,000 and you have $1,100. At the end of the next year your $1,100 is compounded at 10% interest, so your return on investment is $110. Add that to the $1,100 and you now have $1,210. Your interest on $1,210 is $121. So as time passes, your interest amount grows. That is why it is so important that you start now. You have more time for your interest snowball to pick up more and more snow!

Ben and Arthur

Figure 1:B

Both save at 12%. Both save $2,000 per year. Ben starts at age 19 and stops at age 27. Arthur starts at age 27 and stops at 65, and he never caught up with Ben. START NOW!

AGE	BEN INVESTS		ARTHUR INVESTS	
19	2,000	2,240	0	0
20	2,000	4,749	0	0
21	2,000	7,558	0	0
22	2,000	10,706	0	0
23	2,000	14,230	0	0
24	2,000	18,178	0	0
25	2,000	22,599	0	0
26	2,000	27,551	0	0
27	0	30,857	2,000	2,240
28	0	34,560	2,000	4,749
29	0	38,708	2,000	7,558
30	0	43,352	2,000	10,706
31	0	48,554	2,000	14,230
32	0	54,381	2,000	18,178
33	0	60,907	2,000	22,599
34	0	68,216	2,000	27,551
35	0	76,802	2,000	33,097
36	0	85,570	2,000	39,309
37	0	95,383	2,000	46,266
38	0	107,339	2,000	54,058
39	0	120,220	2,000	62,785
40	0	134,646	2,000	72,559
41	0	150,804	2,000	83,506
42	0	168,900	2,000	95,767
43	0	189,168	2,000	109,499
44	0	211,869	2,000	124,879
45	0	237,293	2,000	142,104
46	0	265,768	2,000	161,396
47	0	297,660	2,000	183,004
48	0	333,379	2,000	207,204
49	0	373,385	2,000	234,308
50	0	418,191	2,000	264,665
51	0	468,374	2,000	298,665
52	0	524,579	2,000	336,745
53	0	587,528	2,000	379,394
54	0	658,032	2,000	427,161
55	0	736,995	2,000	480,660
56	0	825,435	2,000	540,579
57	0	924,487	2,000	607,688
58	0	1,035,425	2,000	682,851
59	0	1,159,676	2,000	767,033
60	0	1,298,837	2,000	861,317
61	0	1,454,698	2,000	966,915
62	0	1,629,261	2,000	1,085,185
63	0	1,824,773	2,000	1,217,647
64	0	2,043,746	2,000	1,366,005
65	0	**2,288,996**	2,000	**1,532,166**

Compound Interest Formula: $FV = PV(1 + r/m)^{mt}$

FV = Future Value

PV = Present Value (principal)

r = the Interest Rate--10% is expressed as the decimal .10

m = the Number of Times per year the interest is compounded (monthly, annually, etc...)

t = number of Years (length of time estimated)

The Emergency Fund

The first thing you should save for is the EMERGENCY FUND.

You are saving for the ________________ emergency.
You need a financial umbrella. Sometimes it rains. 75-78% of people will have a negative financial event in the next 10 years.

> "In the house of the wise are stores of choice food and oil,
> but a foolish man devours all he has."
> - Proverbs 21:20 (The Bible, NIV)

The emergency fund is your back up strategy; stored money that you can fall back on when the unexpected happens. The emergency fund takes the sense of urgency out of a situation and allows you to concentrate on the true issue at hand.

You should start with ___________ cash in the bank.
This is the first "Baby Step".

You will eventually work to have ___ - ___ months of expenses in a fully funded Emergency Fund...for most people this will be around $10,000-$15,000.

1.7 Describe 3 benefits to having a Fully Funded Emergency Fund.
1.
2.
3.

You should place this in a __________ ____________ account.

This is for ________________ only and is not a big ___________.

Do not __________ this fund except for emergencies.

The emergency fund is the _________ thing you should save for.
The emergency fund is "Murphy Repellent."

1.8 What is Murphy's Law?

Purchases

Instead of ______________ to buy things use the ______________ fund approach.

For example, if you borrow to purchase a __________ big screen TV and stereo and you do not pay off that "90 days same as cash", you will likely pay an interest rate of ______ giving you payments of ________ per month for ______ months – a total payback of _________.

If you were to save the ______ for ______ months at _____ interest, you would have saved $3,798.
You can get a deal when you use cash.

If you want to buy a $5,000 car, just save ______ per month. Go for the bargain by using cash!

Wealth Building

______________ is the key to wealth building.

You must be ______________ over _________.
Save something every paycheck.

If you save for ______ years, ______ per month, at ______, you will have ______________.

1.9 How much money do you blow per week?

"A little bit steady makes a lot!" Saving a little at a time, each month, is habit forming. It doesn't seem like such a big task when it becomes second nature.

PAC's (Pre-Authorized Checking) help to build in ______________.

Remember that COMPOUND INTEREST is a mathematical ____________.

The rate of return, or _____________ rate, makes the difference.

"Make all you can. Save all you can. Give all you can."
– John Wesley

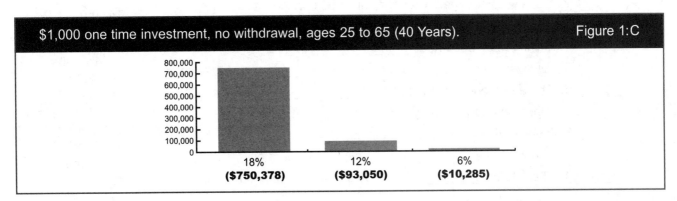

$1,000 one time investment, no withdrawal, ages 25 to 65 (40 Years). Figure 1:C

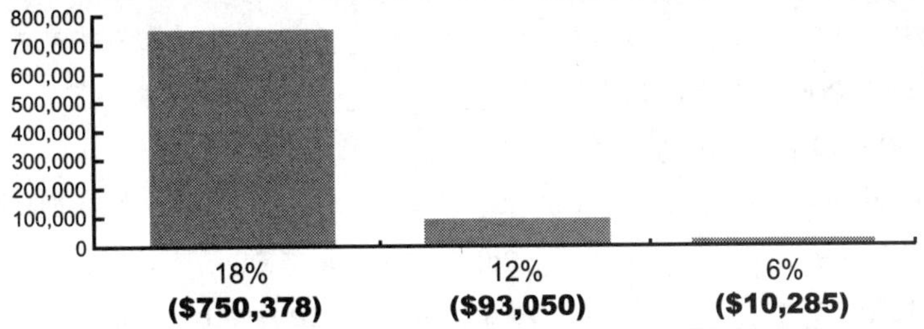

Leave the cave, kill something, and drag it home. If you can't pay for it, you don't deserve it. Change your way of thinking so you won't be broke all of your life.

Money in Review 1

Vocabulary

Define the following terms:

Amoral
Baby Steps
Compound Interest
Emergency Fund
Hoarding
Interest Rate
Money Market
Murphy's Law
PAC
Priority
Sinking Fund

True/False

Determine whether these statements are true or false. If false, change the bold word to make it true.

1. ___ The first thing you should save for is your **retirement fund.** ____________
2. ___ **50%** of people will have a major negative financial event in the next 10 years. ______
3. ___ PAC's help to build in **discipline** with savings. ____________
4. ___ Your first "Baby Step" is to **pay off your debt.** ____________
5. ___ The only difference between saving and hoarding is **attitude.** ____________

Completion

Complete the following statements:

1. With your money you should GIVE, SAVE, and then pay __________.
2. Money is neither good nor bad. It is __________.
3. The emergency fund is for ____________ only.
4. ____________ is the key to wealth building.
5. __________ __________ is a mathematical explosion.

Matching

Match the term with the best statement:

____ 1. Your first "Baby Step" is to put this much in the bank.
____ 2. Save your emergency fund in this type of account.
____ 3. This is what the typical American saves of their after-tax income.
____ 4. Saving must become a __________.
____ 5. A fully funded emergency fund is ________ months of expenses.
____ 6. The emergency fund is not a big __________.
____ 7. When should you pay yourself?
____ 8. Instead of borrowing to buy things, use the ______ fund approach.
____ 9. You will have to __________ either now or later.
____ 10. The rate of __________ makes the difference when saving.

A. First
B. Sacrifice
C. 3-6
D. Last
E. Return
F. $1,000
G. -2.2%
H. 1-2
I. Money Market
J. Sinking
K. Priority
L. Earner
M. Deal

Multiple Choice

Choose the best answer for the following questions:

1. **For most people, a fully funded emergency fund will be about ________.**
   A. $1,000 B. $10,000 C. $5,000 D. $100
2. **After 4 years, $5,000 will grow to how much if it earns 10% interest?**
   A. $7,000 B. $6,550 C. $6,655.50 D. $7,320.50
3. **Which of the following should you save for:**
   A. Wealth Building B. Purchases C. Emergency Fund D. A,B, and C
4. **The typical Japanese saves ______ of their after-tax income.**
   A. 4.1% B. –2.2% C. 7.9% D. 18.1%
5. **Saving is about contentment and ________.**
   A. Pride B. Having money C. Emotion D. Greed

Discussion

1. Why are people not saving in today's society?
2. How much do you think you can save per month?
3. How do you plan on saving this money? Short term or long term?
4. Name some ways you can cut your spending and still accomplish the goals you set out to achieve.
5. Do you need to have an emergency fund at your age? Why or why not?
6. Name an item you wish to purchase in the near future and your goal for buying it with cash.
7. Who has contributed to your knowledge of money? Parents, Teachers, Friends, etc.? Explain.
8. Will you live like Ben or Arthur? Explain.
9. If someone gave you $5,000 today, how would you put it to use?
10. What sacrifices are you willing to make to save money? Why do you think the sacrifices are worth it?

Case Studies

Read the following case studies and write down what you would tell these individuals, if you were their financial counselor.

1. Mark has just received a $10,000 bonus at work and wants to buy a car. He has nothing saved and $7,500 in credit card debt. The car he currently drives is costing him quite a bit of money in monthly repairs. He figures he can buy a nice car and put the money that he saves on repair bills towards his credit card debt, eventually paying it off. What would you tell Mark to do?
2. Diane is about to get a $200 per month raise. She wants a new television and DVD player and would also like to do some home repairs with the extra money. She has $500 in her savings account and figures with her raise she can accomplish her purchases and repairs easily within a few months. She also has $1,000 in credit remaining on her credit card and is considering using it to buy everything now. What would you tell Diane in this situation?

Searching For Savings

C	G	A	L	W	D	C	W	S	V	V	F	Y	O	G
A	B	G	A	A	K	N	Z	E	I	O	C	U	H	N
P	K	Q	C	W	A	K	U	M	A	N	Z	O	U	I
M	Z	I	I	W	A	D	E	O	E	L	A	J	M	K
U	A	R	T	R	E	L	U	G	P	R	T	O	H	N
R	V	V	A	W	O	X	R	O	D	M	N	H	F	I
P	P	F	M	G	L	E	P	I	R	E	O	R	W	S
H	R	Z	E	J	M	V	N	L	Y	R	Y	C	N	P
Y	I	A	H	E	H	G	A	M	O	R	A	L	U	T
E	O	K	T	P	U	R	C	H	A	S	E	S	E	C
M	R	B	A	T	S	E	R	E	T	N	I	K	I	X
O	I	O	M	D	N	U	F	X	E	F	R	O	L	Y
B	T	N	S	N	L	M	W	G	D	A	C	E	N	G
N	Y	V	K	H	F	L	T	A	M	C	V	V	O	P
F	D	I	G	S	V	F	I	W	I	R	Z	V	U	P

AMORAL
EXPLOSION
INTEREST
MATHEMATICAL
PAC
SINKING

COMPOUND
FUND
LAW
MONEY
PRIORITY
WEALTH

EMERGENCY
HOARDING
MARKET
MURPHY
PURCHASES

chapter 2

understanding investments

Objectives:

At the completion of this chapter, you should be able to:

- Explain the KISS rule of investing
- Define "Diversification" and "Liquidity"
- Explain the different types of Investments

Key Terms:

Diversification
Risk Return Ratio
Liquidity
Shares
Mutual Fund
Return

Pocket Change

- According to Thomas Stanley in his book, *The Millionaire Next Door*, the average millionaire has a median income of just $131,000 per year.
- A February 2002, ABC News survey found that 45% of Americans polled falsely believe that diversification is "a guarantee" that investments will do well even if the stock market falls. 63% do not understand the basic concept of inflation.
- *USA Today* states that 39% of Baby Boomers said they would save more and spend less, if given the chance to replan their retirement.

Years ago, when I worked daily in personal sales and later in training sales people, I heard a saying. Most sales people, especially when they are new, talk too much. They talk too much because of their desire to tell the client all the great things about their product or service. Many times a salesperson will talk their client out of the sale by overloading him with information he did not require to make a buying decision.

Salespeople have to learn the art of being quiet at the appropriate time and keeping their pitch simple. With the exception of sales on technical products, people know whether they want a product or not after a reasonable amount of information has been presented to them. We were taught the KISS principle to avoid overcomplicating a presentation. KISS stands for "Keep It Simple, Stupid". We used this bit of comic relief to remind ourselves that it was counterproductive to overcomplicate things. More plainly, it is stupid to make things difficult to understand when they are simple. The handling of money is no exception.

I am not calling anyone stupid, so please don't be offended, but you should remember this basic premise. People will lose thousands of dollars to prove they can invest with the sophisticates. I have had people come into my office who are completely broke, with negative monthly budgets and negative net worths, and then have them argue with me about the interest rate on a particular investment. I am continually amazed at all the broke financial geniuses. Our society has made it a sin to make unsophisticated, uncomplicated investments, but it is all right to have zero savings.

We brag about the investment we made, or the great insurance program we have, and if Harry or Jill at work has a better one it is as if we didn't keep up with the Joneses. Most of us have gotten so focused on the tax advantages, the get-rich-quick scheme, or the sophistication of the investment that we forget to check it against common sense. There is something ridiculously glamorous about investing in something far away with a slick brochure that we don't quite understand. How about exotic bird partnerships with tax sheltered 200 percent returns? Don't laugh; there are more absurd things out there that sell! Some say, "Well, I know what I am doing." How many times have I heard that? They are the ones about to fall the hardest.

This chapter will present a brief and basic overview of different investments and hopefully clarify the KISS principle of money. You must remember, though, that investing in anything more than a savings account should not be done until you have three to six months of expenses for an emergency fund. I am reminded of the old saying that the safest way to double your money is to fold it over once and put it in your pocket.

Investing should not be intimidating. It should be fun and done with confidence and knowledge. You should never invest or utilize a financial plan without trusting your judgment and knowledge on the subject. Educate yourself and ask questions to those who have experience. But above all, when you invest, do it because you know how it works.

Do not let a $3 concept with a $10 word intimidate you.

Keep it ___________ ___________.

It does not mean you are _________ if you do simple investments.
Be wise and keep things simple. Never buy anything over $300 that you do not fully understand!

2.1 A DVD player that can do everything is nice, but more things can go wrong with it! Give some other examples of things that might be better if they were simpler.

Keep in mind, we are not usually conned by con-artists—-we are more often "conned" by well meaning, enthusiastically ignorant relatives and friends.

___________ invest purely for tax savings purposes.

___________ invest using ___________ money.

If you borrow money at 7% to invest in something that may earn 12%, after taxes the 12% looks more like 8-9%. The interest you will pay back on the 7% loan will offset the 8-9% that you "appear" to be earning. If your investment loses money, you are still required to pay back the loan. Stay away from the "games". Keep it simple!

Diversification

Diversification means to ___________ ___________.

Diversification ___________ risk.
(As the old saying goes, "Do not put all of your eggs in one basket—-unless you want scrambled eggs!)

Risk Return Ratio

With virtually all investments, as the ________ goes up, so should the hopeful ___________.

Investments should be for five years or more. Saving is for less than five years. Saving is for things such as a purchases, holidays, etc. Investing is for the long term. With this in mind, you can and should take more risks with investments than with savings.

2.2 Name two things you are currently "saving" for:
1.
2.

2.3 Name two things you will "invest" for:
1.
2.

There are two main risks to look at when investing:

- *You could lose all of your money.* - There are no guarantees with investments, but if you research and pick investments with good track records and diversify, you should be fine.
- *A thing called inflation.* - You need to earn 6-7% at a minimum to keep up with inflation. According to the C.P.I. (the Consumer Price Index), inflation has averaged 4.2% over the last 75 years. So if you are earning 6% on an investment, after taxes the investment looks more like 4.2%. So you have just broke even. Ideally, you want to earn 12-14% to actually make money long term.

Liquidity means the _______________ of your money.

As there is more liquidity, there is typically _________ return.

- Your savings should be more liquid than your investments.
- More risk and less liquidity should bring better returns.
- Less risk and more liquidity bring less returns.

Types Of Investments:

CD's

A CD is a Certificate of ___________, usually at a bank and is just a savings account with a certificate.

With CD's, you are loaning the bank your money and in return, they agree to pay you a small amount of interest. You agree to keep it there for a specified time (6 months, one year, etc.) and they will pay you a higher interest rate than the typical savings account. There is a penalty if you take the money out too soon. CD's and Money Market accounts are suitable for housing your emergency fund.

Compared to other investment options, CD's have a _______ rate of return.

2.4 Other than for the Emergency Fund, why might you get a CD?

Single Stocks

Statistically, with single stocks the average investor will earn only a ____ return over his or her lifetime.

On average, men are more likely to invest in single stocks. The question is why would someone invest in something that is averaging 7% such as a single stock when the stock market as a whole has averaged 12% over the last 40 years. With a single stock, you are not diversified.

With single stocks, there is a ________ degree of risk.

When you buy stock, you are buying a piece or percentage of ________________ in the company.

Your return comes as the ___________________ of the stock increases.

If you buy a share of stock for $50 and the share price increases to $70, you just made a $20 profit per share on your investment. So, if you bought 100 shares of a company at $25, you have invested a total of $2,500. If over time the stock price goes to $32.50 per share, you now have an investment worth $3,250. Remember that the price can go down as well.

You can also earn money from the profits a company distributes called _____________.
(Dividends are usually only issued by companies that are older and more established and can afford to distribute some of the profits to shareholders.)

Bonds

A bond is a ________ instrument where a company owes ______ money.
(A bond is really just a type of I.O.U.)

Your return on bonds comes as the _____________ rates fluctuate.

______ individuals do well with single ________ purchases.
(In terms of risks, bonds are similar to single stocks.)

Mutual Funds

In mutual funds, investors pool their __________ to invest.

Professional portfolio managers manage the pool or ________.

Your return comes as the _________ of the fund is _____________.

What the manager buys tells the type of fund it is. For example, if he or she buys:

- bonds; it is a **Bond Mutual Fund.**
- stock from overseas companies; it is an **International Stock Mutual Fund.**
- stock in companies that are growing; it is a **Growth Stock Mutual Fund.**
- stock in companies that are a little younger and really wild in their growth; it is an **Aggressive Growth Stock Mutual Fund.**

Mutual Fund Tips:

- A mutual fund will contain anywhere from 90-200 different companies in it.
- Yes, you **can** lose money in a mutual fund.
- If you jump in and out of mutual funds you can lose money. **Leave it alone.**
- **97%** of any **5 year** period in the stock market has made money.
- **100%** of any **10** year period in the stock market has made money.

So, look for at least a 5 or 10 year track record – the longer the better. Look also at the **life** of the fund.

Don't panic when the market is down. You need to look at it as a "sale". You are trying to buy "shares". The number of shares you own is very important, so when the price is low, you are able to buy more shares. When the price goes up, you have more shares going up in value and that is where you make your money!

During the Depression, no mutual funds went broke!

_________ -term investments are what you should use mutual funds for.

You should diversify your mutual fund selections as follows:

- 25% Growth and Income
- 25% Growth
- 25% International
- 25% Aggressive Growth

Fund Tips:

- Growth and Income funds are very stable and are also known as Large-cap funds.
- Growth funds are sometimes known as Mid-cap funds and are still growing.
- Aggressive Growth funds are wilder and also known as Small-cap funds.

Even if you are young you should never put all of your money in a Small-cap or Aggressive mutual fund. The ride might be a little too exciting.

Rental Real Estate

This is one of the most non-liquid consumer investments.

As an _______________, this is probably for later in your life.

You should have a lot of _______ set aside, before using this as an investment.

2.5 Why would having plenty of cash be important when using rental real estate as an investment?

Annuities

An annuity is a __________ account within an insurance company.
These accounts are only as safe as the company is strong…so if you have to have an annuity, do not get it with Joe and Tom's Insurance Company, choose a company that is older and more established.

There are both ____________ and ____________ annuities.
A fixed annuity pays you a flat percentage. For example: 6%. If a company can guarantee you 6%, they have to be making more than that to stay in business, so if you are younger, go with the variable annuity if you have the choice.

Annuities grow without having to pay taxes until withdrawal. The problem with annuities is there are several fees attached that you really should not have to pay.

Commodities And Futures

Things such as gold, oil, silver, crops, etc. are examples of commodities and futures.
These are extremely speculative.

These have a _______, very high degree of ________.

You statistically have a better chance in ____________ than you do with commodities and futures.

Avoid trying to get rich quick. The best way to get rich quick is to get rich slow!

Monthly debt payments rob you of your retirement.

Monthly Payments	Years Invested Monthly at **12%** Per Year				
	5	**10**	**15**	**25**	**40**
$100	8,167	23,004	49,958	187,885	1,176,477
$200	16,334	46,008	99,916	375,769	2,352,954
$300	24,500	69,012	149,874	563,654	3,529,431
$400	32,668	92,015	199,832	751,538	4,705,909
$500	40,835	115,019	249,790	939,423	5,882,386
$600	49,002	138,023	299,748	1,127,308	7,058,863
$700	57,168	161,027	349,706	1,315,193	8,235,341
$800	65,336	184,031	399,664	1,503,077	9,411,818
$900	73,503	207,034	449,622	1,690,962	10,588,295
$1,000	81,669	230,039	499,580	1,878,847	11,764,772
$1,200	98,004	276,046	599,496	2,254,616	14,117,727
$1,500	122,504	345,058	749,370	2,818,270	17,647,159
$2,000	163,339	460,077	999,160	3,757,693	23,529,545

On the flip side, retirement can look pretty sweet!

Money in Review 2

Vocabulary

Define the following terms:

Aggressive Growth Stock Mutual Fund
Annuity
Bond
CD
Commodity
Diversification
Dividend
Fixed Annuity
Futures
Investments
Growth Stock Mutual Fund
Large-cap Fund
Liquidity
Mid-cap Fund
Money Market
Mutual Fund
Mutual Fund Bond
Portfolio
Rental Real Estate
Risk
International Stock Mutual Fund
Risk Return Ratio
Savings Account
Share
Single Stocks
Small-cap Fund
Speculative
Track Record
Variable Annuity

True/False

Determine whether these statements are true or false. If false, change the bold word to make it true.

1. ___ **Always** invest for tax purposes. _______
2. ___ **Liquidity** means to spread around and lower risk. _____________
3. ___ Oil and gold are examples of **commodities and futures**. ___________
4. ___ With single stocks, the average investor will earn a **7%** rate of return over his or her lifetime. _______
5. ___ When investing, you should always check the **1-year** track record. _______

Completion

Complete the following statements:

1. Never invest using ____________ money.
2. _______________ means to spread around.
3. The availability of your money is called _____________.
4. Stock profits a company distributes are called ________________.
5. The average mutual fund will have anywhere from ____ to _____ companies in it.
6. You have a better chance in _____ ________ than with commodities and futures.
7. ________% of any 5-year period in the stock market has made money.
8. The average single stock investor will make a _____% rate of return over his or her lifetime.
9. With all investments, as the _______ goes up, so should the hopeful ____________.
10. Never buy anything over $300 you do not fully ________________.

Matching

Match the term with the best statement:

____ 1. Buying a piece of ownership in a company.
____ 2. Investors pool their money to invest.
____ 3. A debt instrument where a company owes you money.
____ 4. A savings account with an insurance company.
____ 5. You should have a lot of cash on hand before investing in this.

A. CD
B. Rental Real Estate
C. Single Stock
D. Mutual Fund
E. Bond
F. Annuity

Multiple Choice

Choose the best answer for the following questions:

1. This type of annuity pays you a flat interest rate with no changes:
A. Variable B. Fixed C. Stable D. Aggressive

2. These are the most aggressive mutual funds:
A. Large-cap B. Mid-cap C. Small-cap D. Global

3. _____% of any 10-year period in the stock market has made money.
A. 50 B. 75 C. 85 D. 100

4. Your piece of ownership in stock is called a ________.
A. Portion B. Share C. Slice D. Cut

5. This is just a savings account with a certificate:
A. CD B. Bond C. Annuity D. Commodity

Discussion

1. Which type of investment would you be most comfortable with? Why?
2. Do you own any investments now? If so, what type and how long have you had them?
3. Does investing in the stock market worry you? Why or why not?
4. If most of the mutual funds crashed, where would your money be safe?
5. Why do you want to look at a LONG term track record with a mutual fund?

Case Studies

Read the following case studies and write down what you would tell these individuals, if you were their financial counselor.

1. John is considering borrowing $20,000 against his home to invest in a series of Aggressive Growth Stock Mutual Funds. The track record for these funds over the last 3 years has been an average growth of 21.2%. The interest rate he will have to pay is only 7.5% so he figures this is a no-brainer. The fact that he is 63 years old is also figuring into his thoughts because he figures he hasn't got very long until retirement. What would you tell John in this situation?
2. Stephanie has just turned 21 and wants to invest 15% of her income into mutual funds. She earns an annual salary of $23,500. She has $22,000 in debt with her car and has no savings. What steps would you tell Stephanie to take?

Risk And Reward

Similar to the TV game show, Wheel of Fortune, fill in the blanks to reveal a message. Letters appear in random order, there is no "code."

A	B	C	D	E	F	G	H	I	J	K	L	M	N	O	P	Q	R	S	T	U	V	W	X	Y	Z
				16																					

___ E ___ ___ ___ ___   ___ ___ E   ___ ___ ___ ___ ___ E   ___ ___ ___
26 16 2 25 8 7   24 2 16   24 14 21 24 8 16   5 2 25

___ ___ ___ ___   ___ ___ ___ E ___   ___ ___ ___ ___ ___ E ___ ___   ___ ___ E ___
25 9 8 13   6 22 4 16 17   12 21 25 3 21 16 17 17   5 2 16 9

___ E   ___ ___ ___ ___ ___ ___   ___ ___ ___   ___ E ___ ___   ___ ___ ___
2 16   17 24 11 18 4 17   2 11 17   9 16 18 4   25 14 24

chapter 3

retirement and college planning

Objectives:

At the completion of this chapter, you should be able to:

- Explain what is meant by "tax-favored dollars"
- List the different types of Retirement Plans
- List the different types of College Funds
- List the benefits of having a Roth IRA

Key Terms:

Roth IRA
Tax-favored
ESA
Qualified Plan
Pre-tax
Rollover
Nest-egg
IRA

Pocket Change

- In the late 1990's, 78% of college seniors graduated with student loan debt.
- According to *Fortune* magazine, the research group Public Agenda estimates that almost 75% of Americans fear they aren't saving enough for retirement.
- *Business Week* reports that only one in four people participate in their 401(k) and only 39% know where their money is invested.
- A June, 2001 NBC News study found that only 3% of US Citizens are saving in any type of IRA.
- Nearly half of all Americans (46%) have less than $10,000 saved for retirement, according to *Miles To Go: A Status Report on Americans' Plans for Retirement,* a new public opinion study released by Public Agenda.

Now that you have a basic understanding of investments, it's time to put some of that knowledge to use. As we mentioned in the last chapter, investing is a great way to build wealth so you can achieve your long-term goals.

According to a Gallup and Robinson survey quoted in *USA Today*, 80 percent of parents perceive college to be either indispensable or very valuable to their child's economic well being, and 31 percent consider it their number-one financial priority. The parents are right: College gives you an advantage in the kind of job you are able to get; however, it is not a necessity. If it comes down to your choosing between saving for your kids' college education and saving for your own retirement, choose your retirement.

According to *Forbes* magazine, by 1993 more than sixty thousand American companies had eliminated their traditional pension plans, to which employees contributed nothing but from which they receive their retirement. That means it is now up to you, the employees, to start saving for your own retirement. As a whole, Americans aren't doing this very well; a May 1995 *USA Today* article reported that only 44 percent of Americans are taking the hint and saving. I guess the other 56 percent are depending on what I call Social Insecurity.

A December 30, 1996, *USA Today* article reported that, in 2029, just as the last of the baby boomers turn 65, Social Security will have only 77 percent of the money it needs to pay benefits. What's more, the U.S. Census Bureau states that 62 percent of Americans retire on incomes less than $10,000 a year. It's time to take responsibility for your future.

You can get over the guilt trip about not paying your kids' way through college. In their book *The Millionaire Next Door*, Dr. Thomas Stanley and Dr. William Danko note that most millionaires in this country put themselves through school. It's not going to kill your kids to have to work to pay for their education. In fact, they may even profit from the experience. If you really want to help, save so you can eat and pay your bills during your retirement and start looking for scholarships for your kids. They will thank you when they can start their adult lives, debt-free and at peace knowing you are taken care of.

Fortune magazine says that almost 75 percent of Americans fear they aren't saving enough for retirement. I have seen the panic-stricken faces of the people *Fortune* is talking about. They are fifty and sixty years old and thought Social Security would take care of them. Now they can barely make it day to day. Don't make the same mistake. Instead, take these three steps to retirement planning:

1. Set goals for your retirement. Think about how you want to live during your retirement years—dream a little.
2. Count the cost. Calculate approximately how much it will take to fund your retirement lifestyle, and set a financial goal that will help you make that dream come true.
3. Create a monthly savings program. Choose the right investments to achieve your financial goal.

Do the details. Most people spend more time picking out their clothes than they do picking out their career, putting together a budget, or understanding their retirement plan. The general vibe throughout the country these days is one of dependence rather than independence: "I'll be taken care of when I'm older... my parents will leave me money...I've got plenty of time to save for retirement." You have to have a game plan in order to win. It is time to educate yourself and put a plan together!

The "Baby Steps" are the steps you should take when establishing a healthy financial plan. The first 3 are critical in avoiding the pains associated with "Murphy's Law". They are as follows:

Baby Step 1: Get $1,000 cash in the bank! This is your miniature Emergency Fund

Baby Step 2: Pay off your debt using the Debt Snowball

Baby Step 3: Fully fund your Emergency Fund with 3-6 months of expenses

You should only begin your retirement planning after you have completed the above 3 steps, especially the emergency fund.

The emergency fund is a key ingredient in establishing a healthy financial plan and should not be overlooked. If you do not have an emergency fund in place, when an emergency occurs, you are more likely to dip into your retirement fund for a quick solution. In reality the penalties far out weigh the rewards and you will end up paying taxes and fees to obtain the money. For example: If you take out $10,000 dollars it will turn into $6,000 due to taxes and an early withdrawal penalty. In effect, you have turned your retirement plan into your emergency fund...not a good idea. Be patient and focused.

Baby Step 4

Invest 15% of your household income into Roth IRA's and Pre-tax Retirement Plans.

Once the Emergency Fund is in place, you should begin Retirement and College funding, which all fall within the long-term investing for ____________ category.

We always want to take advantage of tax-____________ dollars.

IRA

You have a choice. You will either choose the **IRA** or the **IRS.** By choosing not to choose, you have chosen the IRS!

By tax-favored, this means the investment is in some kind of ____________ _________.

This qualifies under the IRS guidelines for some kind of special tax treatment.

There are several types of Qualified Plans.

The __________________ __________________ accounts (or IRA's), the _______________ Employee Pension Plan (or SEPP), and the _________'s, _________'s, and _________'s.

Don't be intimidated by the terminology, these plans are just named after numbers in the tax code books...for example, the 401(k) can be found in section "401", subsection "k". Remember, these qualified plans simply protect your money from taxes.

An IRA is not really an "account", it is an "arrangement". The arrangement is just a "coat" around an investment that will protect it from taxes.

Everyone with _________ income is eligible. If married, filing jointly, non-income earning spouses may contribute as well.

Each person with an earned income can have an IRA of up to _______/_______ per year depending on the year in which you are studying this material.

A non-income earning spouse may also contribute ______/______ more, if married, filing jointly.

In the past, non-income earning spouses could only contribute $250 per year into an IRA. That was penalizing the non-income earning spouse, one of the hardest working individuals on the planet, especially if young children are involved!

3.1 Do you have an earned income? Are you able to start an IRA? Are you contributing?

An IRA is not a _______ of investment.
It is the "coat" around the investment keeping it warm from taxes.

The Roth IRA

Senator William Roth introduced the Roth IRA, during the Tax Relief Act of 1997. This is an "after tax" investment that grows TAX FREE! You have already paid taxes on the money before you put it in the investment; therefore you do not have to pay taxes on it when you take it out.

Again, this is an _______-tax investment that grows tax-free!

Who is eligible?

Singles:

- 100% contribution with income less than $95,000.
- Phase out between $95,000-$110,000. Not eligible above $110,000.

Married filing jointly:

- 100% contribution with income less than $150,000.
- Phase out between $150,000-$160,000. Not eligible above $160,000.

If you are eligible, you _________ do the Roth IRA!

Benefits of the Roth IRA:

1. **The Roth IRA has more _________.**
   You are allowed to take out your contributions, not the growth, without tax or penalty.

2. **You will be in a higher ______________ at retirement if you follow the Financial Peace Principles.**
   If your money is in a Pre-tax retirement plan, when you take it out you have to pay taxes on the money. If you had 4 million dollars in your plan, taxes would be at least one million dollars. However, if your money is in a Roth IRA, it has grown tax free, so the entire 4 million dollars is yours!

3. **You actually will have more __________.**
For example: If you contribute $3,000 into a Roth IRA, you would have to invest about $4,000 into a pre-tax investment to achieve the same outcome because you have yet to pay the taxes on it. Taxes on $4,000 will be around $1,000.

4. **You have a lot more ______________ with a Roth IRA.**

Flexibility:

Tax-free and penalty free withdrawals anytime equal to contributions. This is a fall back if you deplete your emergency fund for some reason.

After 5 years tax free, penalty free withdrawals for 100% if:

- over 59 1/2 years old
- because of death or disability
- first time home purchase (max $10,000)

The SEPP

The ______ employed person may deduct up to _______% of their net profit on the business by investing in a SEPP.

If your net profit on your business is $100,000, you can invest, tax deductible, up to $15,000 into your SEPP. All employees that have been with the firm more than 3 of the last 5 years must receive the same percentage of their pay into a retirement plan if they so choose.

401(k), 403(b), And 457

________ companies have done away with the traditional pension plans.
According to a recent *Forbes* article, 70,000 companies have done away with the pension plan, as most people know it. The message here: You better plan for the future YOURSELF!

401(k)'s and similar plans only work if you participate in them. If you do not put anything in, you will not get anything out!

One of the great things about the 401(k) is that it is portable. If you leave a company, you can take it with you or roll it to another plan.

401(k): found in corporations

403(b): found in non-profit organizations…churches, hospitals, schools, etc.

The 403(b) differs from the typical 401(k) in that, even while you are still on the job, you can transfer the money into another type of investment without triggering the taxes.

457: this is basically a "deferred comp" plan…you have deferred your compensation into it.

Do not use the Guaranteed Investment ____________, or GIC's.
These typically have a low rate of return because the money is in a money market type of investment. You need a better rate of return than 4-6% in order to make money in the long run.

You should be funding your plans whether your company matches or not. The plans that have company matching provide _________ returns.

Pre-tax means that the government is letting you invest the money before you have paid taxes on it. For example: If you make $1,000, it will turn into about $700 after taxes have been taken out. With pre-tax investing, the government is allowing you invest the entire $1,000...including that $300 that you would have been taxed. You get to keep all the interest that $300 earns as long as it is in the account. You just have to pay the government the $300 when you withdraw the money.

Rollovers

You should always roll all retirement plans out to an IRA when you __________ the company.

Do what is called a DIRECT TRANSFER...you do not want the money to hit your hands because at that point it will be taxed and possibly penalized for early withdrawal. A direct transfer is a movement of tax-deferred retirement money from one qualified plan or custodian to another.

You should roll to a Roth ONLY if:

1. **You will have saved over ___________ by age 65.**
   At that point you will be in a higher tax bracket.

2. **You pay your taxes ____________, not from the nest egg.**
   You do not want to crack the nest egg because you want as much money in the account as possible.

3. **You understand that all taxes will become due on the rollover amount.**

Never ____________ on your retirement plan except in dire emergencies.

- You will have unplugged a 12-14% rate of return to pay yourself back 5-7% interest. The math just does not work.
- If you find another job or get downsized, you have 60 days to pay back the loan or the entire amount is considered an early withdrawal and is subject to taxes and penalties amounting to about a 40% hit on your money!
- If you die, that is considered "leaving the company" and your beneficiary has to pay it back within 60 days or is hit with the taxes and penalties.

Federal workers that have the standard thrift plan, put ______% into the "C" plan, ______% into the "S" plan, and ______% into the "I" plan.

"C" is the Common Stock Fund
"S" is the Small Company Fund
"I" is the International Fund

So, we are going to put 15% of our income into Retirement Plans...**Baby Step #4**

1. **If the company matches, take the _________ up to the match. Then do all you can do in _________ IRA's.**
   If that does not take you to the 15%, return to the company plan until you reach the 15% amount.

2. **If your company does not match, start with the ________. If you do not hit the 15%, go to the company plan and finish.**

3. **Complete 15% of income by going to company _______ or SEPP's.**

Just Imagine: A 30-year old couple invests $500 per month in Roth IRA's. That is $6,000 per year. If they earn 12% on their money, at age 70 they will have **$5,882,386 TAX FREE!**

If they leave 4% in the investment, never touch the principle, and just pull off 8%, they will have to live on roughly $480,000 per year!

Baby Step 5 Is College Funding

You should save for college using the Education ___________. This is also called the Educational Savings Account.

You can contribute up to $2,000 per year per child into this account and it grows tax free for college. If a child born today is planning on going to college, the In-state minimum tuition including the necessities will be around $60,000. The ESA should be able to take care of this. There are income limits…these are the same as the Roth IRA limits.

3.2 Using the internet, select 3-5 colleges and check out current college tuition rates. Compare the cost of in-state tuition with out-of-state tuition.
1.
2.
3.
4.
5.

Above the ESA, you should use good _____________ stock mutual funds in an UTMA or UGMA. The UTMA stands for Uniform ______________ to Minors Act.

The account is ________ in the child's name and a _____________ is named. The _____________ is usually a parent or guardian.

Money in an UTMA technically belongs to the child. At the age of 21, they take full responsibility of the money and can use it however they choose, so teach them right!

Many states now offer the _____ plan. This is for people who do not meet certain income limits. The 529 plan allows the fund to basically grow tax-free for college.

There are basically 2 types of plans with the 529:

1. **The "Static" plan allows you to _________ your investments into mutual funds. This is the better of the two.**

2. **The "Age Based" 529 is more conservative. As the child gets closer to beginning college, the investments get less and less aggressive. These have a _______ rate of return. By the time they start school, the investment is practically in a money market account.**

Nevers:

Never save for college using life ______________.
These have a lousy rate of return.

Do not use ____________ bonds for college.

Never save for college using _______ - ________ bonds.

Never use ____________ college tuition.
Your rate of return is the inflation rate for college tuition…about 7%.

Money in Review 3

Vocabulary

Define the following terms:

401(k)
403(b)
457 Plan
529 Plan
Baby Steps
Custodian
Direct Transfer
ESA
IRA
IRS
Nest-egg
Pre-paid Tuition
Pre-tax Retirement Plan
Rollover
Roth IRA
Savings Bonds
SEPP
Tax-favored Dollars
UGMA
UTMA
Zero-Coupon Bonds

True/False

Determine whether these statements are true or false. If false, change the bold word to make it true.

1. ___ You should roll to a Roth if you will have saved **$70,000** by age 65. __________
2. ___ **Pre-tax** means the government is letting you invest money before taxes have been taken out. _____________
3. ___ Savings bonds are a **great** way to save for college. ___________
4. ___ When a child turns **21** they can do what they want with an UTMA. ________
5. ___ The Roth IRA came about in **1994**. _______

Completion

Complete the following statements:

1. You always want to take advantage of ______-_____________ dollars.
2. The _________ IRA is an after-tax investment that grows tax-free.
3. Once the emergency fund is in place, put _______% of your income in retirement plans.
4. You should save for college using the ________.
5. Never __________ on your retirement plan except in dire emergencies.

Matching

Match the term with the best statement:

____ 1. This is a retirement plan for self-employed people.
____ 2. This is a "deferred comp" plan.
____ 3. This is the typical qualified plan found in most corporations.
____ 4. This is a qualified plan for non-profit groups such as schools and hospitals.
____ 5. This is the college fund you would use in addition to the ESA.

A. UTMA
B. 401(k)
C. 457
D. SEPP
E. 403(b)
F. 529

Multiple Choice

Choose the best answer for the following questions:

1. A self-employed person may deduct up to _____% of their net profit on the business by investing in a SEPP.

A. 10 B. 15 C. 20 D. 25

2. Which of the following is NOT part of the "flexibility" of a Roth IRA?

A. Tax-free, penalty free withdrawals after age 59.

B. 1st time home purchase up to $10,000.

C. You can pull out your contributions… sort of a back-up emergency fund.

D. You can buy a car after you have it one year.

3. You should do a ____________ with your retirement accounts when you leave a company.

A. Switcheroo B. Fund Deposit C. Direct Transfer D. Fund Shift

4. You can contribute __________ per year per child in an ESA.

A. $1,000 B. $2,000 C. $3,000 D. $5,000

5. A non-income earning spouse can contribute ____________ the income earning spouse into an IRA.

A. The same as B. $1,000 less than C. More than D. $500 less than

Discussion

1. Why is it important to spread your investments over the 4 categories of Mutual Funds?
2. Why should you wait to invest in retirement funds until AFTER your emergency fund is in place?
3. Why should you always invest in your retirement funds BEFORE you invest in college funds?
4. List some ways you can avoid student loan debt if you do not have a college fund?
5. Why should you take the match if a company gives one before you start a Roth IRA?

Case Studies

Read the following case studies and write down what you would tell these individuals, if you were their financial advisor.

1. Wes and Sue have not saved for retirement and they are in their mid-40's. They are out of debt with the exception of their house and have two children ages 6 and 10. They want to start an ESA to help with college and they have the money to fully fund each ESA. They have $500 in a savings account for emergencies and feel they need to provide a higher education for their children. What would you say to Wes and Sue?

2. Larry and Joan are in their early 60's and are looking forward to retirement. They have all of their retirement funds in Bonds and CD's earning 3-6%. They have no pension plan, and their Social Security payments will be about $1,200 per month combined. The only debt they have is $4,000 on a used truck Larry bought last year. They have $1,000 in savings and are considering using it to pay down the truck. What would you tell Larry and Joan?

I'll Pass On The Dog Food Thanks!

Unscramble each of the clue words. Then, reveal the hidden message, by copying the letters in the numbered cells to the empty spaces at the bottom of the page.

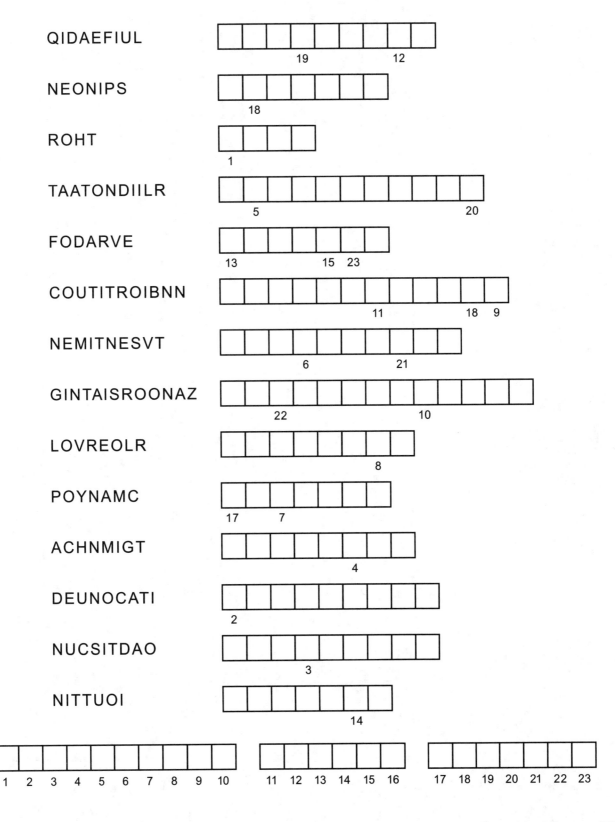

QIDAEFIUL

			19				12	

NEONIPS

	18					

ROHT

1			

TAATONDIILR

	5									20

FODARVE

13				15	23	

COUTITROIBNN

						11				18	9

NEMITNESVT

			6				21		

GINTAISROONAZ

		22						10				

LOVREOLR

						8	

POYNAMC

17		7				

ACHNMIGT

					4		

DEUNOCATI

2								

NUCSITDAO

			3					

NITTUOI

					14	

1	2	3	4	5	6	7	8	9	10

11	12	13	14	15	16

17	18	19	20	21	22	23

unit 2

cash flow planning

dumping debt

relating with money

chapter 4

cash flow planning

Objectives:

At the completion of this chapter, you should be able to:

- Explain why money is active
- Explain why people do not do a budget
- Explain why some budgets do not work
- List the reasons you should do a budget
- Define "Zero-based Budget"

Key Terms:

Active
Debit Card
Budget
Envelope System
Zero-based Budget
Impulse Purchase

Forms:

The following useful forms can be found in the appendix .

Pocket Change

- More than 4 out of 5 adults donate money to non-profit organizations. *
- In 2000, the median amount of money given to non-profits and churches by the typical American was $300. *
- *Forbes* Magazine states that 263 members of the *Forbes 400* are entirely self-made. Their average age is 61 and their average net worth is $3.2 billion.
- According to *Kiplinger's* Magazine, 26 to 30 is the age that affluent individuals typically begin saving for retirement.

* Barna Research 2001

What would you say the chances of success are for a business that keeps no records and does no forecasting of income and expenses? I would say the chances for failure are high, and the chances of success are slim to none. The Small Business Administration says that the number-one reason for small business failure is poor record keeping.

This fact comes as no surprise to most of us, and 90 to 95 percent of American households operate without a detailed, accurate, written outline of income and expenses. They have only a slight clue as to what it takes to keep their household "in business" every month. Not one in 150 people that I have counseled for financial woes have an accurate list of obligations and expenses when they first come to me. No one budgets! To use some overworked expressions: When we fail to plan, we plan to fail...and there is always too much month left at the end of the money.

I have bad news. Everyone needs a written budget. When I say this I hear things like, "A budget, oh no, not me! I am a free spirit!" or "No budget for me—things are pretty well under control" or "Only nerds do written budgets. You know, the guys with the calculators on their belts who don't have anything better to do on Saturday night". Wrong, wrong, wrong.

The word "budget" is a derivative of the French word bougette, a form of bouge, which is a small leather purse. When we discuss budgets we think of small amounts, of stinginess, of a dark room where we can't get out. With these perceptions it is no wonder we don't plan our cash flow on a monthly basis.

We view budgeting as if it is a form of torture. A correctly prepared budget is not a form of torture, nor is it so time consuming that you can't have Saturday night out. On the contrary, a proper, simple, written plan will actually give you more free time and money with which to enjoy it.

I counseled a young single man recently about putting some simple budgeting measures and plans in place. He soon called to say it was as if his money had grown, as if money was coming in from nowhere. Okay, if you don't want to call it a budget call it a "cash flow plan", maybe that won't seem so harsh. But we must implement some written strategies for forecasting and controlling our money.

Developing a budget or cash flow plan doesn't sound like much fun, does it? Does going to Europe, to Cancun to scuba dive, or to Aspen to snow ski—and coming home to face no debt or credit card bills sound like fun? That is what a proper plan will do for you because you can begin planning that debt-free vacation as a part of your plan today. If you are a free spirit and want to have more freedom or time to write or paint, then you can plan financially to attain that status. But until you plan, you will never reach "free spirit" status financially because "unexpected" bills will always clip your wings.

The "Budget"

Oh no, not the budget!

The budget, or the cash flow plan, is one of the most important parts to a healthy financial plan. Without knowing where your money is going, it will be difficult to keep it under control. The majority of people like to feel that they can control certain things, and money should be something everyone strives to control. We are talking about an inanimate object here. The discipline has to come from within.

"If you aim at nothing, you will hit it every time!"
Zig Ziglar

"A cash flow plan is people telling their money what to do instead of wondering where it went!"
John Maxwell

Money is ___________.

Money is always moving. That's why it is called "currency". The odd thing about currency is that it tends to leave those who can't control it and flow to those who can. So you see, you will either learn to manage money or the lack of it will always manage you!

Author Stephen Covey states that the number one habit of effective people is that they are "pro-active", meaning they happen *to* things. You have to be the one to set the tone. You are the boss when it comes to your money, so you have to delegate the way the money works. You have already taken your turn at working for the money. Now it's the money's turn to work for you!

You need to do a written ___________ ___________ plan, monthly.

This is a BIG job, but so is eating an elephant! You might be able to eat that elephant if you take it one bite at a time. That is how you do a budget – a little at a time – and before you know it, it's done! Do not get discouraged if it doesn't work out the first few times. You can expect to mess up in the beginning. Be persistent and stay the course.

If you were going to build a $160,000 home, you would definitely get a set of blueprints. You would want everything to work out – the floor plan, the structure, and of course the cost. With the average income in America being just over $40,000, this house would represent four years of work. Well, if you are going to get a blueprint for the house, set up a blueprint for the lives that are in that house. A budget is just a blueprint – a set of plans to make things run smoothly.

You need to keep your ___________ balanced.

This does not mean bringing the total down. Make sure that you account for every deposit and expense by reconciling your checkbook with the bank statement as soon as it arrives. By doing this, you will know the exact amount of money available to you.

Checking Tip:

Reconcile your bank statement with your account within 72 hours or receiving it in the mail. Don't procrastinate!

Bounced checks are a sign of crisis __________.

Some people say that bouncing a check is "no big deal." It is a huge deal, when you consider that most bad check fees run $20-$30 each. Hmm...Let's see...$25 dollars per month at 12% interest over 40 years would be $294,119.31!

If you need to, use __________ checks.
These types of checks will help you if you are one of those people who tend to forget to enter checks in the check register after writing them.

Another budget buster is the _______ card or the ________ card.

It is extremely easy to use the debit card when you are short of cash. The problem with using this card is that statistics have shown that people spend upwards of 12% more when they pay with "plastic." The expense does not emotionally register the same as cash transactions. These cards are also easy to use when you want to impulse. You really have to be careful.

4.1 What are some ways you can avoid the "impulse" purchase? What is the last thing you purchased on "impulse" and did you regret the purchase soon afterward?

Reasons People Do Not Do A Budget:

1. **It has a __________ and _________ connotation.**
   Many people feel like they can't do what they want to do if they have to abide by a budget. This is not the case at all! You can still spend what you want, but the difference is that you are now doing it on purpose. Once you have given every dollar a name, you tend to be more careful in your spending.

2. **A budget has been used to _________ you.**
   If you were ever in a position of wanting something and were told over and over again that "it's not in the budget, it's not in the budget!" After awhile, you would despise the word "budget". Not only that, you might resist ever getting on a budget!

3. **You never had one that really __________.**
   If you leave something out of the budget (and you will for the first few you draw up), when the time comes that the category in question pops up...the budget crashes. For example, if you had not budgeted for home maintenance and repairs, when the hot water heater starts spraying like a fountain you might throw up your hands and say, "a budget doesn't work!" You have to account for "real life" because hot water heaters are "real life"!

4. **Paralysis from _________ of what we will find.**
   It could be that we really do not want to know how much we are actually spending at restaurants every month. This is called DENIAL.

4.2 Name one reason why you do not want to do a written cash flow plan.

Cash Flow Plans Do Not Work Because:

1. **You __________ things ________.**
   Make sure that you account for every possible category.

2. **You ______________ your plan.**
   When you set up a budget, do not make it so complicated that you (or your spouse) have to get an interpreter to decipher it. Make it simple to understand and you will be a lot better off. It is also a good idea to "write" the first few budgets down on paper…and by "write", that means by hand. Stay away from the computer…use a pencil and paper!

3. **You do not actually _____ one.**
   That will bust your budget every time!

4. **You do one, but you don't _______ on it.**
   The entire reason you were doing a cash flow plan was to take control of your financial situation. If you write it out but don't live on it, why did you do it in the first place? That would be like renting a movie you know you won't watch…what's the point?

Reasons We Need A Cash Flow Plan:

1. **It removes the management by __________ from your finances.**
   If you know going into the month that all of your necessities are taken care of, the stress level goes way down. When you set up your budget you need to prioritize. The first five things you should budget for, after giving and saving, should be food, shelter, clothing, utilities, and transportation. Yes, you need to pay off any debt you may have, but paying Visa while you or your spouse or your children go hungry is absurd!

4.3 List 3 things you budget for consistently.
1.
2.
3.

2. **Managed money goes ___________.**
   You will feel like you got a raise when you begin to take charge of your money!

3. **For those who are married, it will remove many ___________ from your marriage.**
   When you are married, the first few budgets you work on will result in an argument or two to say the least. After awhile, through this increase in communication, you will become closer than ever before. Once you agree with your spouse about money, the level of trust increases and stress decreases.

4. It will remove much of the ________, ________, and ________ that is some times associated with necessities purchased such as food.
You actually begin to worry less when it comes to needs…and you also find there are things you thought you needed, but now you realize those things were "wants".

5. It will remove the ________ ________, which will definitely remove the ________ in your life.
Just knowing that you will have the proper amount of money in your accounts to cover the expenses that you incur will be a tremendous burden lifted off of your shoulders. Stress is a killer…let's do all we can to eliminate it!

6. A written plan, if actually lived and agreed on, will show if you are ________ ________ in a certain area.
You would be amazed to find out how much money you blow without even realizing it. Shopping at the grocery stores and especially the convenience markets will eat a budget alive if you do not have a grip on it.

4.4 Track your spending for a week and determine how much money you actually spend. Were you aware of how much money you were spending on frivolous items such as drinks from the vending machines? How much would that be in a year if you were to total it up? You might be surprised.

Cash Flow Tips:

You need to do a ________ -based budget.
When you sit down to write out your budget, list your after tax income that you have to work with …this would be your "take-home" pay. Prioritize your expenses and list them out on paper. Do not pay cable before you buy food!

Give every dollar a category or a "name". If you think you are finished and you have money left over, you still need to assign it to a category, otherwise it will just "disappear". Once you have listed your expenses, INCOME minus OUTGO should equal exactly zero. That is a zero-based budget. Remember…there is never a perfect month and your expenses will vary accordingly. This is real life, so plan for the unexpected car repair or late night pizza run.

Implement the ________ system.
This is one of the best money managing systems around! Take some of your monthly expenses and fund an envelope to pay cash when you make your purchases. For example…food, gas, and clothing would be three good categories to start with. If you spend $200 per month on food, put $200 in an envelope and buy nothing but food from that envelope. If you get paid twice a month, put $100 in the envelope on your two paydays and live on that amount. This will take some adjusting, but over time you will hit on just the right amount needed to fund all of your cash envelopes. This is a great way to meet your financial goals. Try it for saving, too.

4.5 What categories would you fund envelopes for? Why? Start an envelope for something you plan to purchase in the next 6 months or for an upcoming trip.

Money in Review 4

Vocabulary

Define the following terms:

Active
ATM Card
Budget
Check Card
Currency
Debit Card
Discipline
Envelope System
Impulse Purchase
Persistent
Pro-active
Procrastinating
Reconcile
Zero-based Budget

True/False

Determine whether these statements are true or false. If false, change the bold word to make it true.

1. ___ You need to do a **zero-based** budget. ____________
2. ___ You have to pay interest on **debit card** purchases. ______________
3. ___ A budget **will be** the same each and every month. ______________
4. ___ You need to reconcile your bank statement within **2 weeks** of receiving it. ___________
5. ___ Other than saving and giving, you should first budget for food, clothing, transportation, shelter, and **retirement**. ______________

Completion

Complete the following statements:

1. Money is moving. That is why it is called ______________.
2. _____________ _________ are a sign of crisis living.
3. Managed money goes _____________.
4. The _____________ system will help you control spending on things such as food and clothing.
5. Many people do not want to do a budget because they think it has a ________________ and _____________ connotation.

Matching

Match the term with the best statement:

____ 1. Paying this before buying food is absurd.
____ 2. This is buying without thinking.
____ 3. Happening "to" things is being ___________.
____ 4. To balance your checkbook back with the bank.
____ 5. This is another name for a cash flow plan.

A. Inactive
B. Reconcile
C. Budget
D. Impulse Purchase
E. Credit card
F. Pro-active
G. Strict Money Guide

Multiple Choice

Choose the best answer for the following questions:

1. **To manage money effectively, you need a:**
   A. Checkbook B. Budget C. Lot of money D. Computer
2. **You should do a written cash flow plan every:**
   A. 3 months B. 6 months C. 2 months D. month
3. **A budget will remove:**
   A. Money fights B. Stress C. Guilt D. A, B, and C
4. **You should never _____________ your budget.**
   A. Overcomplicate B. Leave things out of C. Adjust D. A and B
5. **Bounced checks are a sign of __________ living.**
   A. Normal B. Crisis C. Elaborate D. B and C

Discussion

1. If you had an irregular income, how would you set up a cash flow plan that would work?
2. Should you set up a cash flow plan? How would this help in spending and saving habits?
3. If you know you can afford your expenses without writing out a plan, why do you need to do a cash flow plan?
4. How old should you be when you start using a cash flow plan?
5. What are the things you will need to budget for after you graduate—when you begin college or go to work full-time? List at least 5 and explain each.

Case Studies

Read the following case studies and write down what you would tell these individuals, if you were their financial advisor.

1. Jim and Eileen make a combined income of $42,200 and are having trouble making all of their payments. They have two new cars with payments totaling $652 per month and 3 credit card payments totaling $325 per month. They are renting and want to buy a home, but they are afraid they will not be able to afford more than the $600 per month in rent they are already paying. They are also afraid that at the rate they are going they will get behind in their payments and eventually lose any eligibility to get a home loan. What advice would you give Jim and Eileen?
2. Terry and Gwen have just had a baby girl and want to start a college fund for her. Currently they are just making ends meet with their $38,000 income. They need to find an extra $167 in their budget to begin saving in a fully funded Educational Savings Account. They have zero debt except their home and are putting 15% of their income into Retirement Plans. What are some things they can do to their budget to find an extra $167?

Go With The Flow

C	A	R	B	O	N	R	B	V	F	P	D	O	O	F
E	P	O	L	E	V	N	E	O	W	R	C	A	Y	U
U	T	I	L	I	T	I	E	S	E	O	U	D	N	R
C	Y	E	T	B	Y	B	T	G	K	C	R	A	O	G
T	I	S	O	P	E	D	A	K	I	R	R	Z	E	T
E	Y	L	R	Y	R	N	P	O	M	A	E	K	M	F
R	N	O	I	T	A	T	R	O	P	S	N	A	R	T
G	E	I	D	M	V	N	W	B	U	T	C	D	V	C
T	N	C	L	E	T	L	C	K	L	I	Y	E	L	H
H	E	I	O	P	B	V	D	C	S	N	V	C	E	E
T	C	G	H	N	I	I	Y	E	E	A	B	N	V	C
H	X	J	D	T	C	C	T	H	L	T	S	A	I	K
I	M	J	H	U	O	I	S	C	Q	I	I	L	T	R
E	A	O	C	O	B	L	L	I	Z	N	R	A	C	E
S	H	E	L	T	E	R	C	E	D	G	P	B	A	D

ACTIVE
CARBON
CLOTHING
DEPOSIT
FOOD
PROCRASTINATING
TRANSPORTATION

BALANCED
CHECK
CURRENCY
DISCIPLINE
IMPULSE
RECONCILE
UTILITIES

BUDGET
CHECKBOOK
DEBIT
ENVELOPE
MANAGE
SHELTER

chapter 5

dumping debt

Objectives:

At the completion of this chapter, you should be able to:

- List the different ways people get into debt
- Compare the "Credit Card" vs. the "Debit Card"
- List the 6 steps to get out of debt
- Explain how the Debt Snowball works

Key Terms:

Paradigm
Co-signing
Lease
Credit Card
Debt Snowball
Debit Card
Tax Deduction

Forms:

The following useful forms can be found in the appendix.

- The Debt Snowball page 168
- Pro-Rata Debts page 169
- Sample Pro-Rata Letter page 171

Pocket Change

- 64% of households under the age of 30 have a net worth of less than $25,000.
- 65% of college students have credit cards.
- 28% of students roll over debt each month.*
- 40% of Americans say they are living beyond their means, primarily due to credit card debt, according to the Lutheran Brotherhood in 2001.
- 70% of households under the age of 30 have credit cards according to *USA Today*.
- 49% of households under the age of 30 have car debt. The average amount owed is $12,600 according to *USA Today*.
- 31% of young adults ages 18-19 have a credit card in their name.*
- Today's college students who have student loans leave college owing an average of $12,000 in student loan debt.*
- According to the Federal Reserve, total consumer debt topped $1.5 Trillion in January 2001.

*Jumpstart Coalition for Financial Literacy

Avoid the lifestyles of the rich when you are not rich. I have learned that the best things in life, including good "stuff", come only at the expense of personal discipline. Many of my suggestions do not appear "fun" in the short run, but in actuality they are a lot more "fun" in the long run. Henry David Thoreau once observed, "Almost any man knows how to earn money, but not one in a million knows how to spend it".

You must limit your style of living. You must figure out what your actual income is and then proceed to live far below that mark. You may respond, "That is impossible!" No it is not impossible; difficult, maybe, but not impossible. It will take some time to undo some of the messes you have gotten into—and this book will help you—but it is very possible.

Experts have tracked the baby boomers' financial growth and spending habits for years. What they have found is that although most couples are broke when they get married, within three or four years they have attempted to copy their parents' net worth and lifestyles. Author Larry Burkett notes that with the broad spectrum of borrowing available, many young couples can quickly have almost the same lifestyle that it took their parents twenty-five years to achieve. These couples drive the same cars and live only blocks away—except they may have a newer house and nicer clothes than their parents, who make more money and have worked a lifetime to attain these possessions. The only problem is that the new couple has covered themselves with every imaginable type of debt, and their financial ship is very unsteady. Why? Because they could not say "no" to themselves.

We Americans have become a nation of servants to financial institutions. We used to joke that a bank was where you could borrow money if you could prove you didn't need it. Now, with the advent of aggressive credit marketing strategies, we can borrow even when we shouldn't be allowed to. We are sold credit in so many ways by so many people that we end up buying a lot of it, meaning we borrow money. We borrow money because we are sold on the convenience, perceived prosperity, and fun that all that "stuff", and associated debt, are supposed to bring us.

I mean, we are getting in deep. *Consumer Reports Money Book* states that the typical household debt totals more than $38,000. In addition, *Consumer Reports* says we have over 1 billion pieces of plastic with one of the major cards in 74 percent of all households. You are weird if you don't have a credit card; that is definitely market saturation.

You have to remember to slow down! You must evaluate carefully your purchase decisions because if you will sacrifice for a few years, you can live easier later. Instead, if you strap yourselves to all these lifestyle purchases to live well, you actually cause an ongoing cancer that will prevent you from ever living well.

Dump debt. If you don't, remember you are instantly a servant to the lender.

You Have To Get Out Of Debt To Live With True Financial Peace!

There are a series of myths about finances that need to be addressed.

If a __________ is told enough, it becomes accepted as __________.

Debt is dumb, and you do not have to go into debt to win. Many people feel that the only way to prosper is to finance "stuff". This will not bring you true happiness. There is not enough "stuff" to make you happy!

Debt is a product that has been __________ to us so aggressively since the 1960's that to imagine living without debt requires a complete paradigm ________.

Your paradigm is your set of glasses. It is the way you perceive the world. If you see or hear something enough, you begin to accept it as fact. There are a lot of things out there in today's society that many people accept as truth. The TRUTH is you CAN live without debt, and you WILL prosper along the way!

Credit History

1910 – In the Sears catalog credit was called "folly"!

J. C. Penney would not allow credit to be given in his stores while he was alive. It wasn't until after his death on February 12, 1971, that credit was widely accepted in J.C. Penney stores.

Henry Ford hated debt so much that he made Ford Motor Company wait 10 years before they could allow credit to their customers.

1950 – Diner's Club launches their charge card in the United States.

1951 – Diner's Club issues its first credit card to 200 customers. The card could be used at 27 New York City restaurants.

1958 – Bank of America mailed out 60,000 applications to its customers offering the Bank Americard.

1958 – American Express was born.

1970 – 15% of Americans carried credit cards.

1970 – Standards established with the credit card magnetic strip enable the credit card to flourish.

1976 – The "Bank Americard" changes its name to VISA.

1986 – Sears, after much squabbling with VISA, created the Discover Card. This became the most profitable division of Sears.

According to Sears' annual reports, the company has made more money over the last five to ten years from credit card interest than they have with the sale of merchandise.

In the year 2000, there were over 4.2 billion credit card solicitations mailed throughout the country. Did you get one?

You have to understand that debt is a product. It is like anything else that is sold. The problem is the typical consumer does not look at debt as a product but as a way to move up in the world. This "moving up" is an illusion more than anything else. We want others to feel we are successful, so we finance the world to prove to them that we are. The next time you are at a traffic light, count all the newer model cars that you see. Do you actually think they are all paid for? It is the old "keeping up with the Jones's" mentality. We have got to learn to be happy with what we have so we can be content with who we are!

There Are Myths About Money, And There Are Also Truths. Here Are A Few Of Each.

Myth: If I loan money to a friend or relative, I will be __________ them.

Truth: Loaning a friend or relative money will cause the relationship to be strained or __________.

"The rich rule over the poor, and the borrower is servant to the lender"
Proverbs 22:7 (The Bible, NKJV)

If you lend someone money, whether it be a friend or relative, you are placing that person in bondage. If you borrow money, you are placing yourself in bondage. The friend or relative relationship changes. You will not treat each other like you used to...especially if someone is late making payments!

Myth: By co-signing a loan, I am __________ a friend or relative.

Truth: The bank requires a co-signer because the person isn't likely to __________.

Co-signing for someone is very dangerous to your finances because if they do not pay, you have to take care of the debt yourself. If the bank or other lender, who is aggressively marketing debt, will not loan them money, there must be a problem somewhere. You, on the other hand, know them well and trust them to pay so you co-sign…DANGEROUS. Do not loan them money or co-sign for them. If you have the money, GIVE IT TO THEM! Tell them the only thing they have to do to pay it back is to give to someone else down the line.

Myth: Cash advance, rent-to-own, title pawning, and tote-the-note lots are needed __________ for lower income people to get ahead.

Truth: These are horrible, __________ rip-offs that are not needed and benefit no one!

Myth: Playing the Lotto or other forms of gambling will make me __________.

Truth: These things are a tax on the poor and a tax on people who can't do __________.

The majority of people that are in these lines are not from wealthy neighborhoods. You do not see a line of Jaguars when you pull up. Most people seem to think that there is a "get rich quick scheme" right around the corner. The fact is, the best way to get rich quick is to get rich over time.

The average American spends anywhere from $25-$40 per month on the lottery. If you take the average of this (about $32) and invest it at 12% from age 20 to age 70 – your working lifetime – you would end up with **$1,249,866.87** every time.

5.1 Name something you could do without. How much does this cost per month?

5.2 If you took the amount in **5.1** and invested it, how much would it total in a year? Using the Monthly Retirement Worksheet in the Appendix (p. 142), calculate the total of your investment after 30 years.

Myth: Car ____________ are a way of life.

Truth: Staying away from car payments by driving reliable used cars is what the typical millionaire does. That's ___________ they became millionaires.

We ARE what we drive. At least that is the way we feel sometimes. You have got to avoid placing so much emphasis on a material thing. Cars are nice, but the average car payment in this country is $378 over 55 months. If you were to take that same $378 and invest it at 12% over 40 years, you would have 4.4 million dollars!

5.3 What kind of car would you like to own? How much will it cost you? How much per month? Is it worth it?

Used Car Costs

These five vehicles lost a larger-than-average portion of their resale value, yet continue to offer above average reliability, according to *Automotive Lease Guide*.

Make & Model	Current Price of 1998 model	Depreciation since 1998	Price of Brand New 2001 Model
Audi A6	$16,943	56%	$34,400
Ford Expedition XLT	15,400	50	29,975
Infinity QX4	20,632	45	35,550
Land Rover Discovery LSE	19,750	52	36,350
Toyota Avalon	17,000	45	30,305

*Note: All vehicles feature four doors and where available, four-wheel drive. Current prices of 1998 models are estimates and assume average mileage and clean condition.

Sources: Automotive Lease Guide, Edmunds.com, Money Magazine

Myth: ____________ your car is what sophisticated people do.

Truth: The car lease is the most _____________ way to finance and operate a vehicle. If you own a business, you do not need to lease a car for the tax advantages. A _________ - ______ car can still be used as a business deduction by using mileage or straight-line depreciation.

Remember, at the end of a lease, you have nothing to show for it. You have to turn the car in! *Smart Money* Magazine did a study and found that the typical new car sale for cash nets the dealer only about $82 nationally. If you finance it, the profit increases to about $775 per car. If you LEASE it, the profit jumps to $1,300 per car. When you see car commercials, what are dealers pushing the most? The LEASE! Naturally they are going to push what will net them the most money! They are in business to make money, your money!

In order to minimize the money lost on things that go down in value, buy slightly ________ letting someone else take the hit with the depreciation.
Buy a 2 year old or older car with low mileage!

Myth: I can get a good deal on a _______ car.

Truth: A new car, according to *Kiplinger's Personal Money Management* Magazine, will lose ________ of it's value in the first 4 years.

A $28,000 car will lose $16,800 in value in the first 4 years you drive it. That means that after 4 years the car is worth $11,200! You have lost $350 in value per month driving that thing. If that is not sickening enough, had you financed it you would be paying interest on top of losing the value…a double hit!

New Car Costs

Depreciation and interest charges account for more than half the annual costs of owning and operating a vehicle.

Depreciation/ Interest	50.4%	Tires	4%
Fuel	19%	License	0.6%
Insurance	13.3%	Other	3.7%
Maintenance	9%		

*Percents based on costs associated with a typical intermediate-size vehicle.

Sources: Runzheimer International/USA Today

Myth: The Home Equity Loan (HEL) is good because of the __________ deduction and is a substitute for the emergency fund.

Truth: You don't go into _____________ for emergencies and a tax deduction is not good ____________.

Tax deductions are fine if you have them but you do not go into debt to create them. For example, if you borrowed $50,000 at 10% interest, you would pay $5,000 per year in interest. If you make $65,000 per year, you can deduct the $5,000 in interest you paid that year, meaning you pay taxes on $60,000 instead of the original $65,000. If you are in a 25% tax bracket, and you had to pay taxes on that $5,000 you deducted, you would have paid $1,250 in taxes. So let's see…pay $5,000 in interest to avoid paying $1,250 in taxes…hmmm…

If you want a tax deduction, give to the church or other charitable organization and you get the same deduction without the debt.

Myth: I will take out a 30 year mortgage and I promise I'll pay ________.

Truth: Life happens, and things come up. Never take out more than a ____________ fixed rate loan.

The FDIC did a study and found that 97.3% of people do not systematically pay off a 30-year mortgage. The intentions are there but you have to quit lying to yourself. Besides, a 15-year mortgage is not that much more expensive!

— Let's say you borrow $80,000 for your home at 10% interest.
— If you borrow for 30 years, your payments are $702 per month.
— If you borrow on a 15-year mortgage, your payments are $859 per month.
— You are paying an extra $157 per month with the 15-year mortgage

But...

— With a 30-year mortgage, you will pay back $252,740!
— With a 15-year mortgage, you will pay back $154,743!
— This is a savings of 15 years in payments and **$97,997 in INTEREST!**

Myth: It is ________ to take out an Adjustable Rate Mortgage or a Balloon mortgage because I know I will be moving.

Truth: You will be moving when they ______________.

This is an extremely bad deal because you are gambling on interest rates when they are down already...you need to ALWAYS do a FIXED rate mortgage!

Myth: You need to take out a credit card or car loan to build your __________.

Truth: Open credit card accounts with zero balances and car payments count against you when qualifying for a home _____________.
With open credit card balances, you are an accident looking for a place to happen. Anytime you cut up your credit card, call the card company and close the account to future charges so no one can get access to your information.

Myth: You need a credit card to _______ a car.

Truth: The _________ card will work at all major rentals. Be sure to check in advance.
If they do not accept the debit card they are probably too expensive anyway!

Myth: You need a _________ card to check into a hotel, to make purchases by phone, or over the web.

Truth: The __________ card will do all of the above.

Myth: I pay mine off every _________.

Truth: 78% of Americans do not pay off their credit cards every _______.

A recent Dunn and Bradstreet _____________ reports that when you spend cash you spend less.

On average, you will spend 12-18% less when spending cash than when using plastic. If you are buying food, you will spend 40-60% less by spending cash. One other thing…never buy groceries when you are hungry. Can you imagine how much money you would spend if you went to the store while you were hungry and then to top it off, use plastic to make your purchase?

Myth: I'll make sure my ___________ gets a credit card so he or she can learn to be responsible with money.

Truth: Teens are the #1 ___________ of credit card companies today.
USA Today notes that Citibank, the largest issuer of VISA, will spend 100 million dollars this year just marketing to high school and college students. There is something about being the first card owned by a consumer that creates a sense of what is called "brand loyalty". You feel attached to the company that gave you your first card.

5.4 Have you gotten any credit card offers? If so, what was the credit limit?

Myth: Debt consolidation __________ money and you get one smaller payment.

Truth: Debt consolidation is a ________.

Debt consolidation typically saves _________ or no interest because you throw low interest loans in as well. You can't borrow your way out of _________ and smaller payments actually equal more time in _________.

Myth: Debt properly used is a _________ and it will help you create prosperity.

Truth: Debt is proof that the borrower is slave to the ___________.

When surveyed, _____ of the *Forbes 400* say that becoming and staying debt free is the number one key to building wealth.

If you did not have any payments, how much could you _______, how much could you invest, how much could you blow, and how much could you ___________?

Steps Out Of Debt:

Quit ____________ more __________!
You can't get out of a hole while you are digging out the bottom!

You must __________ money.
Discipline is the key to saving!

Sell _____________.

Part-time ________ or overtime.

Use the Debt ____________.
(See worksheet, p. 168)

Money in Review 5

Vocabulary

Define the following terms:

Balloon Mortgage	**Debit Card**	**Lease**
Co-Signing	**Debt Consolidation**	**Myth**
Credit	**Debt Snowball**	**Paradigm**
Credit Card	**HEL**	**Tax Deduction**

True/False

Determine whether these statements are true or false. If false, change the bold word to make it true.

1. ___ The FDIC found that **56.9%** of people do not systematically pay off their 30 year mortgage. _________
2. ___ The **new car sale** nets the dealer the most profit. _____________
3. ___ Debt is a product that has been aggressively marketed to us since the **1960's**. ________
4. ___ Sears created the **Mastercard**. ________________
5. ___ The Adjustable Rate Mortgage has rates **that vary** based on the current interest rates and is not a good idea. ____________

Completion

Complete the following statements:

1. If a myth is told enough, it becomes accepted as ______________.
2. The __________ is a tax on people who can't do math.
3. The average car payment is $________ per month for _______ months.
4. You should never take out more than a ______ year mortgage.
5. The average car will lose _____% of its value in the first 4 years.
6. A tax ________________ is not good math.
7. The ___________ is the most expensive way to finance a car.
8. In 1970 only ________% of Americans carried plastic.
9. Your ____________ is the way you see the world.
10. The first plastic arrived in the form of the __________ _________ card.

Matching

Match the term with the best statement:

____ 1. Number of credit card offers mailed out in 2000.
____ 2. Borrowing money using your home as collateral.
____ 3. To combine debt into one payment.
____ 4. Taking responsibility for some one else's loan.
____ 5. Changed it's name to VISA in 1976.

A. Lease
B. BankAmericard
C. Discover
D. 4.2 Billion
E. 5.7 Billion
F. Debt Consolidation
G. HEL
H. Co-signing

Multiple Choice

Choose the best answer for the following questions:

1. **Which is the best way to buy a car?**

   A. Lease B. Purchase New C. Used (2 years or older) D. Fixer Upper

2. **This company made more on the sale of credit than they did on the sale of merchandise over the last 5-10 years:**

   A. Sears B. Wal-Mart C. J.C. Penney D. Target

3. **The effective yield on some Rent-to-Own products is about:**

   A. 400% B. 1,800% C. 1,200% D. 600%

4. **What percent of Americans do not pay off their credit cards every month?**

   A. 55% B. 62% C. 70% D. 78%

5. **You will spend _________ more on purchases when you use plastic instead of cash.**

   A. 10-20% B. 8-15% C. 12-18% D. 15-25%

Discussion

1. Why do people go into debt when they know that they will have to pay more for an item once they figure in interest?
2. Why are teens a major target in the credit card industry?
3. You have just paid off your car but it needs some repairs. Should you fix it up and take a chance on lots of repair bills in the future or buy a new car?
4. What is the best way to avoid feeling like you have to use credit and how will you approach credit offers you receive as you get older?

Case Studies

Read the following case studies and write down what you would tell these individuals, if you were their financial advisor.

1. Janie is getting married very soon. She and her fiancé want to buy a home but she is unable to qualify for a mortgage due to her bad credit. He cannot qualify due to his low income. His parents are willing to co-sign as they are very well off and want to help get them started on their new life together. What would you tell this young couple?

2. Mike has a relative that has a terminal illness and he let him use his credit card. This relative has already put over $4,000 on this card and shows no sign of stopping. Mike is scared. He wants to know if he should ask for the card back or just ride out the storm considering his relative's condition? What would you say to Mike?

Shark Alert!

F	T	C	D	D	J	D	D	F	N	O	B	O	N	M
Q	I	R	O	N	T	A	E	C	O	E	B	O	E	O
L	A	N	J	S	B	K	N	B	I	H	I	W	Q	R
C	L	U	A	O	I	O	S	P	T	T	E	U	U	T
E	K	A	R	N	O	G	A	L	A	C	C	R	I	G
O	S	R	B	L	C	Y	N	I	D	H	N	N	T	A
P	O	A	L	W	M	E	C	J	I	T	A	K	Y	G
W	N	A	E	E	O	E	S	G	L	Y	V	U	D	E
R	B	V	N	L	R	N	D	C	O	M	D	X	G	X
A	Q	T	R	P	V	U	S	F	S	U	A	I	B	H
B	S	F	E	R	E	S	P	O	N	S	I	B	L	E
N	S	D	C	R	E	D	I	T	O	H	T	U	R	T
E	M	I	T	R	E	V	O	P	C	O	C	A	S	H
D	L	Z	S	R	X	R	Y	Q	K	E	U	I	Y	Y
E	B	I	J	L	W	G	U	U	G	Z	C	V	K	Y

ADVANCE
CARD
COSIGN
DEPRECIATION
LEASE
OVERTIME
SNOWBALL
BALLOON
CASH
CREDIT
EQUITY
MORTGAGE
PAYMENTS
TRUTH
BORROW
CONSOLIDATION
DEBT
FINANCES
MYTH
RESPONSIBLE

chapter 6

relating with money

Objectives:

At the completion of this chapter, you should be able to:

- Explain the general differences that exist between men and women as they relate to money
- Describe why you should pay commissions instead of allowances to children
- Explain the benefits of doing a budget together when married

Key Terms:

Value System
Accountability
Commissions
Envelope System
Debt Free Fund

Pocket Change

- Scripps Howard news service is quoted in *The Detroit News* as saying that "statistics show that as many as 70% of divorcing couples attribute the breakdown of their marriage to arguments over money."
- Marriage counselor, Gary Smalley identifies 5 behavioral differences concerning men and women in his book, *Making Love Last Forever.*
    1. Men love to share facts, women love to express feelings.
    2. Men connect by doing things, women connect by talking.
    3. Men tend to compete, women tend to cooperate.
    4. Men tend to be controlling, women tend to remain agreeable.
    5. Men tend to be independent, women tend to be interdependent.

Money is a major part of family dynamics. It plays more of a major part than most of us want to admit. I have observed that the families who have good control of their money seem, by that same strength of character, to have strong families that raise children who are contributors to society. That is not to say that good families do not have financial problems, because many of us have, but the same strong character qualities that raise and run strong families protect people from a lifetime of financial problems.

Money—how it is handled and how it is managed—plays an intense role in the dynamic of the family. It contains this dynamic, not because of its intrinsic value, but because the flow of money represents the value system under which that family operates. In husband and wife relationships or relationships with children (teenage and above) the flow, control, and management of money is a real point of pressure.

Only an ostrich, with his head buried, would say that money is not a major issue in family life as we begin this century. Almost all divorces list financial problems as the reason, if not one of the major reasons, for "irreconcilable differences". Most husband and wife teams have such a limited knowledge of basic household financial principles that they are afraid to even discuss the issue. In a recent *Worth* magazine poll, couples surveyed said the number one thing they fight about is money.

It is time for all of us to grow up enough to quit thinking that we are the "John Wayne" of our finances. You do not have the corner on all the knowledge of the financial world, nor do I. You cannot ride in on your white horse, make snap decisions, implement quickie strategies, and still be ready for the next commercial. Our financial lives are more complex in this time than the consumer or even the professional investor can fully comprehend on his own. The man, woman, or couple who make significant financial decisions without careful consideration of outside counsel first is destined for pain and heartache.

The very first place counsel should be sought is in your home. Yes, your spouse does have a brain and one that may even work better than yours. The traditional sexist relationship where the wife is not involved in matters of money is not only shortsighted, it is also just plain dumb. On the other hand, the "modern" woman who allows her husband to completely dump all the finances on her is not only being mistreated, she is also missing out on basic opportunities of communication in a good marriage. Do you think these are strong statements? Well, how is it supposed to be? I normally see that one of the two partners is naturally more adept at handling numbers and keeping up with budgets, and I believe that person should do so. It doesn't matter whether this person is the man or the woman. That person should keep the records, but that person should not make all the decisions.

Any time one member of a marriage is making most or all of the financial decisions without the consultation of the other, the basic communication of the marriage is lacking, and this couple is usually headed for financial problems. It is just common sense: two heads are better than one.

Personal Finance Is About 80% Behavior And Only 20% Head Knowledge.

The flow of money in a family represents the ____________ ____________ that family is operating under.

Your treasure is where your heart is!

Where and how you spend your money says a lot about who you are. Look at your check register and you will find this is true. Your value system is what you deem as important in life.

6.1 Name some of your values in life and some of the things you value...are there any similarities or consistencies? Explain:

Men, Women, And Money:

With The Emergency Fund:

Men: "Boring...not sophisticated ______________."

Men feel that the money in an emergency fund could be earning more interest. They feel that the money could be put to much better use, but in reality if they will just set this money aside and only touch it for emergencies, it will relieve a tremendous amount of stress on the woman's side of things. Her level of trust will increase and this will strengthen the marriage.

Women: "The most ______________ key to our financial plan.

Having 3-6 months of expenses set aside only for emergencies gives women a comfort zone they can get no other way. If a medical situation arises or something in the house breaks down and has to be replaced, knowing that there is money enough to fix it gives her an inner peace that cannot be accurately described.

With Shopping:

Men get good deals by ______________. Men want to win!

Men want to feel that they have beaten the competition. Men generally do not like to shop. They may go, but they get tired very quickly. When most men go into a store, they know exactly what they want, they get it, and they are gone...home to watch the ballgame!

Women get good deals by ______________. Women enjoy the process of looking for the deal.

Shopping is a BIG deal to a lot of women. They really enjoy the day! Not only is this a stress reliever in some cases, but also women look at shopping as if it were a TREASURE HUNT! They know the deal or treasure is there somewhere and they want to be the one to find it!

With Financial Problems:

Men lose ________-_________, because with men money usually represents a ______________.

Men often times feel beaten down when money problems arise. They feel that they have let the family down and criticism at this point could cause worse feelings. What is really needed in this case is encouragement. Let him know that the family believes in him…that is critical at this stage of the game.

Women face _________ or even __________, because usually with women money represents ____________.

Women need reassurance that everything will be fine. Several hugs and smiles will go a long way in restoring her faith and taking away some of the fear she is constantly feeling in the midst of this crisis. She needs to know that the marriage will survive, and that you will hold on to her. Her biggest fear at this point is will the financial struggles lead to more problems that can't be repaired. Do not let something such as money take away one of the greatest gifts you could ever receive…your spouse!

Bankruptcy and Divorce are best friends!

Marriages And Money

The #1 reason people file for divorce in North America is _________ ___________.

Author Larry Burkett suggests that money is either the best or the worst area of communication in a marriage.

As you learn to discuss major purchases and budgets together, you begin to agree on your _______ __________.
You are now a TEAM!

As you agree on your value system, you are going to see a huge change in your relationship. It is important to understand that in most cases opposites attract. That being the case, one of you is hot and the other cold. One is on time and the other late. One is a saver and the other a spender. If you can work together and agree on your budget, you are agreeing on your values, goals, passions, fears, and priorities. And that is the union you need to work toward!

6.2 Are you a spender or a saver? How do you know this?

When this happens, you will reach a ________ in your marriage that you can experience no other way.

Who Does The Financial Decision Making?

Both, ________, __________!

The partner with the natural ________ can prepare the __________, but the ultimate decision making should be done by _________.

Combine the strengths and weaknesses you both possess to formulate a plan. Do not rely on one person's judgment on things. Remember, opposites attract. Let that attraction work for you instead of against you for a change.

The "________" likes to do the budget...the "________ spirit" feels controlled!

The nerd likes to take control. They feel that they are doing the free spirit a favor by taking care of them. The problem is, the free spirit does not really want to be taken care of.

The free spirit can't understand why the nerd does not want to go out and play. The free spirit feels that everything will work out fine. Just give it time!

When it comes time for the nerd to submit the budget to the free spirit for review, the free spirit laughs in the nerds face for trying to be controlling..."a budget, huh?"..."yeah, right!"

Here are some rules for the "budget meeting":

NERDS:

1. When you submit the budget, understand that you have had your say...now, shut up!
2. This is a meeting, not a summit (10-20 minutes max).
3. Let the free spirit win sometimes or they might not come back!

FREE SPIRITS:

1. Come to the meeting!
2. Talk at the meeting. Give input.
3. Never say, "whatever you want to do, honey".

Children do what feels good. Adults devise a plan and follow it.

Singles And Their Money

Time _________ (no time) and fatigue can lead to poor money management.

Beware of __________ buying, which can be brought on by _________ or even the "I owe it to _________" syndrome.

52% of the single moms live below the poverty level!

Single parents have to do ALL of the jobs typically divided among two people. It can be very tempting to let impulse take over just out of convenience when you are tired...for example, eating out when it would be less expensive to eat at home.

A written plan gives the _________ person empowerment, self-accountability, and _______________.

Develop an _________________________ relationship.

This would be someone to discuss major _____________ with, before you make the purchase.
If this is someone who tells you that all of your purchases are o.k., then this might not be a good accountability partner.

This would also be someone to discuss your __________ with.
These people need to love you enough to let you know when you are making a bad decision, whether it is financially based or not.

Teach The Children

The teaching of fiscal responsibility is not the __________ responsibility. This is _________ responsibility!

Pay ____________________, not allowances.

Do not make allowance for the children. Make them responsible. Give them several chores to do around the house and pay them for what they do. If they don't do the chores, they don't get paid. Children also need jobs around the house they do not get paid for. They do these chores as part of their responsibility within the family. But if you don't take advantage of the opportunities to teach kids work ethic with money attached, they may never learn.

Words are ___________.

If you __________ you eat, if you don't _________ you don't eat.

Teach by ____________.
What you do speaks a lot louder than what you say!

Show them how to live _________ free and how insurance, IRA'S, and other financial matters work.

Do not be afraid to let your children see the money coming in and going out of the household. Explain to them how the money gets in the accounts so things can be paid. Also explain what the money is spent on so they will have a better appreciation for the things they have. They need to see that there are limits to the amount of money that comes in.

If the children are young, use a clear ______________ as a savings bank. Children are very visual learners and this will enable them to see their money grow.

When the children are ages _______, use the envelope system to keep track of the money.

This system helps children to understand that there are three things that can be done with money: giving, saving, and spending. Teach them the importance of all three.

Explain that they need to put money into the _________ envelope so that they can learn the power of giving.

Somewhere around ______ - ______ years old, help your kids open a checking account.

6.3 Do you have a checking account? How old were you when you opened it? What is its function?

Let your children save for buying their own _______.

You may match what they save dollar for dollar to motivate them. They may appreciate the car more and take better care of it if they have their own money invested in it.

6.4 Name something you saved up for yourself. Did the fact that you worked for it change the way you looked at the purchase?

What if you got yourself in a position where, not only could you do a ____________ fund, but also have a _________ _________ fund for your children?

A debt-free fund is the type of fund that you could set up once you have accumulated some wealth. You should have wealth if you follow these principles and that wealth could change your entire family tree. With this fund, when your children get married, you could give them a paid for house, provided they agree to avoid debt and put the equivalent of a house payment into investments so that they could accumulate some wealth. Imagine the peace that marriage would experience. No money problems! That marriage would have a better than average chance of succeeding, to say the least.

Money in Review 6

Vocabulary

Define the following terms:

Accountability
Allowance
Checking Account
College Fund
Commission
Debt-free Fund
Empowerment
Envelope System
Fiscal
Free Spirit
Negotiate
Nerd
Self-esteem
Time Poverty
Value System
Work Ethic

True/False

Determine whether these statements are true or false. If false, change the bold word to make it true.

1. ___ When children are **8-10** years old, help them open a checking account. __________
2. ___ Let your children save for buying their own **car**. _____________
3. ___ You need to get a **shopping** partner to discuss your major purchases with. __________
4. ___ When children are **3-5** years old, teach them the envelope system. ______
5. ___ The teaching of fiscal responsibility is **your** responsibility. _______

Completion

Complete the following statements:

1. ______% of single moms live below the poverty level.
2. The partner with the natural gift can prepare the budget, but the ultimate decision-making must be done by _________.
3. Men get good deals by _____________.
4. Women get good deals by __________.
5. With women, money represents _____________.

Matching

Match the term with the best statement:

____ 1. The #1 reason people file for divorce in this country is __________.
____ 2. Pay children ____________, not allowances.
____ 3. The ___________ says "everything will work out".
____ 4. You need to teach by ________.
____ 5. With young children, use a ________ container to save money.

A. Clear
B. Nerd
C. Free Spirit
D. Sturdy
E. Commissions
F. Example
G. Money Fights
H. Lecturing

Multiple Choice

Choose the best answer for the following questions:

1. Who should do the financial decision making in the home?

A. Men B. Women C. Both D. The children

2. The ______ likes to do the budget.

A. Nerd B. Free Spirit C. Child D. Wife

3. A "budget meeting" should last __________.

A. 1 hour B. 45 minutes C. 2 hours D. 10-20 minutes

4. Men lose _________ when it comes to financial problems.

A. Hope B. Self-esteem C. Sleep D. Their temper

5. The flow of money in a family represents the ___________ that family is operating under.

A. Guidelines B. Budget C. Habits D. Value System

Discussion

1. What advantages do singles have when it comes to finances? Disadvantages?
2. In a marriage, why should a budget be agreed upon by both partners?
3. What were you taught about money?
4. Do you receive commissions or an allowance?
5. How would you set up your envelope system?

Case Studies

Read the following case studies and write down what you would tell these individuals, if you were their financial advisor.

1. Meryl is having a hard time convincing her husband to sit down and do a cash flow plan. He is the spender, and she is afraid he is going to spend all that they make. He is working 70 hours a week, and their household income is only $29,000 per year. That income is from his full-time job as he spends his part-time job money on his entertainment. He feels that with his extra job, he should be able to spend that money however he chooses. They have credit card debt and some minor medical bills. Meryl wants to get out of debt but her husband says everything is fine. What would you tell Meryl?
2. David and Melissa want to teach their 18-year old son how to handle money responsibly. The young man has no interest in going to college, but wants to go to work so he can make money to "party". His car was a Christmas gift, and he only pays for gas as David and Melissa pay for the insurance, which amounts to $1,500 per year. They are afraid he is going to flunk out of high school if he doesn't get his priorities in order. He does not seem to be worried. What would you say to David and Melissa?

Teach The Children

Unscramble the tiles to reveal a message.

.	EN	NOT	LL	N T	WAY	HE	IS
D I	SH	AND	OUL	HE	PAR	UP	HIL
IN	O,	HE	IT	D G	T F	DE	TRA
A C	WH	HE	OLD	WI	ROM		

unit 3

buying only big, big bargains

buyer beware

understanding insurance

chapter 7

buying only big, big bargains

Objectives:

At the completion of this chapter, you should be able to:

- Explain why you should be honest when negotiating
- List the 3 keys to getting bargains
- List the 7 basic rules of negotiating
- List places you can find great deals

Key Terms:

Integrity
Win-Win Deal
Negotiating
Walk-away Power
Patience
Mark-Up

Pocket Change

- Where Americans Shop

62.4% of Americans shop at discount stores.

22% shop at conventional stores.

15.6% shop at national chains.

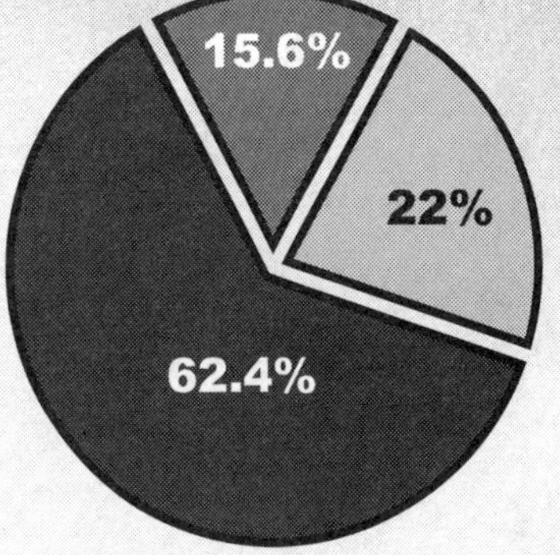

Source: USA Today

You must understand three essential things to hunt big game, and "big bargains": you must learn to negotiate; you must learn where to find bargains; and you must have patience. We will discuss each one in detail.

You must learn to negotiate everything. Everything you buy is negotiable at some time, at some place, and you must find it. The days of impulse buying are over, and the days of negotiation are in for the people who want to get control of their financial lives.

Most people are very anti-confrontational by nature. Most of us, even the boisterous and outgoing, do not want head-to-head confrontation. If you understand that people do not want to meet head-on, it will aid you in your negotiations. If you will approach your purchase looking for a way to win for everyone, you will buy things very cheaply. If someone needs to sell very badly, you have helped him by making that purchase. But you must win too, and your winning can occur in the area of price or terms.

You must negotiate with everyone. Two major pizza chains in our area are competing aggressively for their share of the market. My family prefers the taste of one brand better, but the other brand runs better advertised specials. My wife was determined to get the brand we wanted at the other's price, so when she called to place the order she told our brand they would have to match the other brand's price if they wanted the business. At first they did not want to, because there was a good bit of price difference, but when my wife explained that she would simply call the other brand and place an order, they gave us the good pizza at the good price. Our family does this just for the fun of it.

I do not buy a car stereo from the showroom floor. I want them to bring the one from the back with a small scratch, and I will save $200. I buy kitchen appliances, cars, clothes—everything—at a discount, simply because I have the nerve to ask.

If you have ever visited a foreign country you know that haggling in the marketplace is a way of life for all the rest of the world. But, not us. Oh, no! We have to go to the shining shopping mall and pay full retail with markup plus, and we charge it at 18 percent interest or we are not happy. It is time to change! We must start today to do things differently.

You can have some great fun in this area of getting great buys. The more great buys you get, the more fun you will have, and the more confidence you will have in these principles. I will not tell you that these great buys are on every corner, but if you will work at negotiating, hunting buried treasure, and having patience, you will change your cash outflow dramatically. When your cash outflow is decreased, you can save even more. Then you can get even better buys. And you can save more, and so on goes the spiral of financial peace. Go for it!

It Is Proper To Get A Great Deal If You:

1. have in no way ________________ the truth.

If you are lying, you are sacrificing your integrity to get a deal. There is no bargain out there worth compromising your integrity for, so be honest and tell the truth. When you tell the truth, people know it and they are going to be more willing to help you out.

2. have not set out to __________ the other party.

Is your intent to do damage to someone or to someone's business? Where is your heart when in the negotiating mode? Keep in mind, the person you are bargaining with needs your business, but not at the expense of losing theirs.

3. have created a win-______ deal.

When negotiating, do what you can to save yourself money *and* put the other person in a position that they can benefit.

7.1 Discuss a situation where you created a Win-Win deal in a negotiating situation.

In most areas of the world, negotiating is a way of life. Here in this country, however, we get in our lease car, drive to the shopping mall, and use our credit card with the 18-22% interest rate just so we can get 10% off during the "SALE"!

Some people get embarrassed when they ask for a bargain, but it's better to be embarrassed than broke! Wealthy people learned to negotiate a long time ago, maybe that's why they are wealthy. They ask for a deal and many times they get it. If they don't, they leave with their money. It's your money, you need to be careful with it and don't be afraid to be picky when it comes to the price.

The First Key:

The first key to being a "Big Time Big Game Bargain Hunter" is you must negotiate ________________.

Just because you are in a retail establishment does not mean the people will not negotiate with you. There is something called a "mark-up" on items and there is some room to move the price around. Many times, you will have to deal with someone other than the clerk (i.e., a manager or owner), if you want to negotiate the price. Ask who is in charge and speak with that person; typically, they are more concerned with the flow of money in the business than the part-time employee.

7.2 Have you ever bargained in a retail store? Explain:

Don't feel bad about getting a good deal, unless you've been dishonest. Just because you've received a deal does not mean you've taken advantage of someone. The bottom line is that they get some of your money and you get the product or service at a reasonable price.

Win -________ really works, so don't be ____________ to ask for the ___________!

The Seven Basic Rules Of Negotiating:

90% of winning a negotiation is gathering information on what the other person's needs, wants, fears, and passions are. If you gather information, you win!

1. Always tell the absolute __________.

Dr. Thomas Stanley, author of *The Millionaire Next Door*, did a study and found that 87% of the people with a net worth of ten million dollars are first generation rich. In other words, these people went out and became wealthy on their own. He also found out that the number one characteristic that these people possessed was a high level of integrity.

2. Use the power of ________.

Cash is _______________.

Cash is _______________.

(Don't just say "I'm going to pay cash"...take out the cash and let them see it.)

Cash has ____________________.

At this point the deal is done. People are more likely to take cash (and less of it) if they know that they will have the money in hand. You are no longer a risk to them. They have your money and don't have to wait for a check to clear or see if you have enough credit available to settle the debt.

3. Understand and use "Walk-away ___________."

When you don't have "walk-away power", you have very little, if any, leverage. You have to maintain a distance with the items you wish to purchase, otherwise the people selling to you know that you are "hooked" and will be less likely to negotiate with you.

4. __________ up!

Silence is one of the most powerful, pressure oriented things in a negotiation or conversation. The trouble is, we do not like the silence and we want to jump right in and negotiate price...just be quiet.

5. Say "That is not _________ enough."

If you will say this and then just "shut up" you'll be surprised at the amount people will come down on the price. With this technique you are not saying anything about price…you are letting the seller do all of the price-cutting themselves.

This technique is frequently used by collectors who are trying to get your money…don't play their games. So, be aware that these techniques may be used on you and not always in a proper way.

6. ___________ guy, ________ guy.

This is a technique used primarily against you. For example, on the car lot, the salesman will not negotiate price but he will have to go talk to the "manager". He will then give you the routine that the manager will not go for the deal but he is doing all he can to help you out. You are being played and you need to talk to the manager yourself or "walk away"!

7. "If I give..." The take _________ technique.

Just before you close a deal tell the seller, "If I give this, I want you to throw in something".
For example, if you buy a DVD player, have the store throw in a free DVD movie to go with it.

The Second Key:

The second key to being a "Big Time Big Game Bargain Hunter" is you must have ______________.

Don't get ____________ to a purchase.

With this type of patience, "walk-away power" is accentuated! Wait for the sales…drive around and look for cars that have been out on the front lawn for two months. If you are married to a purchase, everybody knows it!

The Third Key:

The third key to being a "Big Time Big Game Bargain Hunter" is you must know where to find the __________.

One other thing you can do to get a good buy is to _________ something of value, goods or ____________.

Many times you have something someone else would like to have. Use this when you are wanting to get something. You may need new tires and you could strike a deal with a service station owner to give him something he wants in a trade.

You could buy some blank gift certificates and give yourself as a gift…free baby-sitting or yard-work. It will mean a lot because you are giving of your time.

7.3 Give an example of how you've traded for an item or how you've given of yourself in place of a gift.

Places To Find Great Deals

1. ______________________________
These are basically glorified yard sales with more items and slightly higher prices.

2. ______________________________
Individuals are more interested in getting rid of an item than they are making a profit. They need the money more than they need the item.

3. ______________________________
Be careful at auctions if you do not know what you are doing. Look over the items before you bid. You can get great deals but you can also get bad ones.

4. ______________________________
Clip only the coupons for things you would buy anyway. You can save hundreds of dollars per year on food if you coupon properly.

5. ______________________________

6. ______________________________

7. ______________________________
These are great places to buy cars and other repossessed items…caution should be observed as you need to investigate what you are buying if at all possible.

8. ______________________________
This is when you send in proof of purchase to get free gifts or cash back.

9. ______________________________
This is a great way to buy real estate if you have the patience.

10. ______________________________
No…everything in a pawn shop is not stolen!

11. ______________________________

12. ______________________________
If you have children, this is the place to buy clothes…you can buy for a lower price, let them wear them for a while, then sell them at consignment for almost what you paid for them. They're practically FREE CLOTHES!

One other thing you can do is find a convention that is closing down.

At the closing of a convention, if there are items the merchants have to pack up and ship home, they may be willing to sell it cheap or even give it to you to avoid the hassle. **ASK!** You never know what you will get unless you ask.

Money in Review 7

Vocabulary

Define the following terms:

Auction
Bargain
Consignment Shop
Couponing
Estate Sale
Foreclosure
Integrity
Pawn Shop
Refunding
Repo Lot
Walkaway Power
Win-Win Deal

True/False

Determine whether these statements are true or false. If false, change the bold word to make it true.

1. ___ You must learn to negotiate **some things**. ______________
2. ___ When negotiating, you should not set out to **harm** the other party. _____________
3. ___ You can get great deals if you find a **convention** that is closing down. _____________
4. ___ **Silence** is one of the most powerful, pressure oriented things in a negotiation. __________
5. ___ **50%** of winning a negotiation is gathering information on what the other person's needs, wants, fears, and passions are. ________

Completion

Complete the following statements:

1. You must not misrepresent the _________ when negotiating, or else you will compromise your integrity.
2. Use the power of ________ when negotiating.
3. Don't get ______________ to a purchase.
4. You need to know where to find the __________ when looking for bargains.
5. You can _________ something of value if you do not have the money in a negotiation.

Matching

Match the term with the best statement:

____ 1. This technique was once very popular with car dealers.
____ 2. A great place to buy cars.
____ 3. This is a place where you bid on items you wish to purchase.
____ 4. Glorified yard sales with slightly higher prices.
____ 5. This is an excellent place to buy children's clothing.

A. Auctions
B. Estate Sales
C. Repo Lots
D. Foreclosures
E. Good guy, bad guy
F. Flea Market
G. Consignment Shops
H. Manipulation

Multiple Choice

Choose the best answer for the following questions:

1. **When negotiating, set up a ________ deal.**
   A. Win-win B. Slick C. Modest D. Profitable
2. **Which is not a characteristic of cash:**
   A. Visual B. New C. Emotional D. Immediate
3. **One of the best places to negotiate is at ___________.**
   A. Yard Sales B. The mall C. The grocery store D. Sears
4. **___________ have no profit margin when selling an item.**
   A. Discount houses B. Used Car dealers C. Individuals D. Malls
5. **Sending in "proofs of purchase" to get discounts and cash back is called:**
   A. Refunding B. Couponing C. Wholesaling D. Retailing

Discussion

1. What are some of the reasons you refuse to negotiate?
2. Name some bargains you have gotten over the years.
3. Why is it important to tell the truth when in a negotiation?
4. Discuss why this country has moved away from negotiating?
5. Why do you feel that negotiating is so important in other parts of the world?

Case Studies

Read the following case studies and write down what you would tell these individuals, if you were their financial advisor.

1. Janine is wanting to buy a friend's car but does not have the amount that they want. They are wanting $3,000 for the car and she only has $2,500. She is considering borrowing the extra $500 from her sister to purchase the car. She feels that she may be able to get the price down if she tells them that she is wanting the extra $500 for some dental work she is considering. She doubts she will have the work done, but feels that this might be a good negotiating technique to save some money. What should Janine do in this case?
2. Sarah and Derek are about to have a baby and need a baby bed. They see one at a yard sale that is within their budget, but feel that using someone else's baby bed is in bad taste. They are afraid that their friends will think they are cheap if they buy used things for their baby. They are on a tight budget, but they are considering a retail store to find something newer. How would you handle this situation?

Bargain Bonanza!

Unscramble each of the clue words. Then, reveal the hidden message, by copying the letters in the numbered cells to the empty spaces at the bottom of the page.

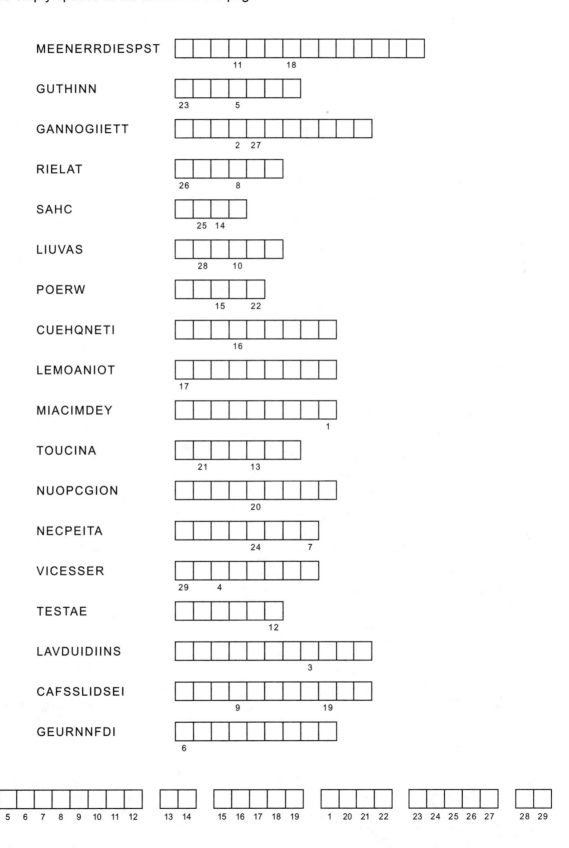

MEENERRDIESPST	11 18
GUTHINN	23 5
GANNOGIIETT	2 27
RIELAT	26 8
SAHC	25 14
LIUVAS	28 10
POERW	15 22
CUEHQNETI	16
LEMOANIOT	17
MIACIMDEY	1
TOUCINA	21 13
NUOPCGION	20
NECPEITA	24 7
VICESSER	29 4
TESTAE	12
LAVDUIDIINS	3
CAFSSLIDSEI	9 19
GEURNNFDI	6

1 2 3 4   5 6 7 8 9 10 11 12   13 14   15 16 17 18 19   1 20 21 22   23 24 25 26 27   28 29

chapter 8

buyer beware

Objectives:

At the completion of this chapter, you should be able to:

- List the 4 major ways companies compete for your money
- Explain what is meant by "Opportunity Cost"
- List the 5 steps that will help you in a "Significant Purchase" buying decision

Key Terms:

Financing
Significant Purchase
Buyer's Remorse
Opportunity Cost
Finite

Pocket Change

- According to the Consumer Federation of America, average annual interest rates for 14-day "Payday Loans" range from 213% to 913%.
- *Kiplinger's* Magazine reports that 9.5% of Americans do not have a bank account.
- In 2000, more than half of all new vehicles sold (approx. 17.7 million) were financed according to the *New York Times*.
- CNN/FN states that $21,009 was the average price of a new car in 2000.
- A report from *USA Today* stated that Volkswagen has the youngest average-age car buyer at 38.
- In 2001, *USA Today* reported that General Motors created, iSYS (for innovative Smart Youth Strategy) a team of designers, engineers and marketing executives studying what kids as young as 6 might want in a car.
- According to *USA Today*, Toyota has a specific group called, Genesis, that focuses on creating new marketing and sales strategies focusing on 20 to 30 year olds.
- *USA Today* stated in 1999, 8.8% of new vehicles were bought with cash.

In the 1970's when I started in the real estate business, I learned the Latin phrase *caveat emptor*, which means "let the buyer beware". The context was residential real estate in which the seller of the property normally pays the real estate commission. Since the seller is paying the agent, the buyer technically has no representation, so he should "beware". In this age of governmental bureaucracy we assume that as consumers someone or some agency is always watching out for us. We take that for granted, and, in truth, we are reasonably sheltered from actual scams and/or dangerous products.

However, we are ignorant as to how much effort, time, energy, and money is spent to get our business and thereby our money. While companies spend billions of dollars and hours to sell to us, we sit idly by, getting sold and sold and sold. And many families buy themselves into financial ruin. If you ever are to get control of your financial life you must learn to "just say no" to buying.

We must develop a power over purchase instead of allowing our purchases and the people from whom we make the purchases to have power over us. We must remember that we can always spend more than we can make. I once met a man whose annual income in one year increased from $42,000 to $175,000. Both years he spent everything he made. He had no sales resistance, no power over purchase.

For me to label every honest company or person who wants to sell you something "the enemy" may seem overstated, but in fact it can be the enemy of your financial peace of mind. As consumers, we must quit being so lazy in making purchase decisions; we are often sold goods and services by juvenile tactics and strategies.

Good salespeople know a customer who asks a question about the product or service is giving what is called "a buying signal", so the salesperson will just turn on the pitch that much more. For example, a good car salesperson will not just answer yes or no to a question like "Do you have that car in stock in blue?" Instead he will answer you with "If we do, would you rather finance that on forty-eight or sixty months?" And when you answer that question you are much closer to buying that car.

This is not a game! It is how these people make a living and if they are not good at persuading you to spend your money on their product or service, they simply starve out of the business. So the sale is very, very important to them. The sale is also important to their company, which also makes a profit. Of course, I am not implying that a good salesperson can make us go into a hypnotic state in which we lose all willpower; I am saying we need to wake up! Good salespeople are a reality, and they do have a substantial impact on your purchasing decisions, especially if you are unaware and/or are mentally lazy.

You must develop power over purchase rather than letting the purchases have power over you. Remember this definition of a rich man—-a person who is not afraid to ask to see something cheaper.

We live in the most marketed to culture in the history of the world!

Profile Of The Enemy

This Is The Enemy Of Your Financial Peace!

Companies use every angle to aggressively compete for your _________.

Companies need to make a profit or they will quickly be out of business. Therefore it is extremely important that they aggressively go after your money. Sales people that do not cost-justify their positions will soon be out of a job.

American Demographics reported in 1971 the average American had 560 advertisements presented to them per day. By the year 2000 the number had grown to over 4,000 advertisements seen per day. Why the increase? Retailers know that advertisements make an impact. Otherwise they would not spend millions per year on advertising budgets. Advertising and marketing is a big deal.

We are consumers, and we are consuming at a rate that is greater than what we are producing. As a matter of fact, a recent study reported that between 60-70% of the United States GNP (Gross National Product) is based on consumer spending. We just can't say NO.

The 4 Major Ways Companies Compete For Your Money:

1. **_______________ selling**

   This is the one-on-one sale. If you are thinking about buying an item over $300 there always seems to be someone around to "assist you"! They have a tremendous impact on you as they are trained to sell and they do an excellent job at it. Most salespeople are trained to answer a question with another question.

   For example: Visit a car lot and ask, "Do you have that car in blue?" their response might be "I think we do. Would you like to put it on 48 or 60 months," thus leading you to the purchase.

2. **_________________ as a marketing tool.**

   If a salesperson can make it easy for you to buy, chances are, you'll be more likely to make the purchase. The down side is money you will lose in interest.

   For example: In a furniture or electronics store, you might be asked, "Would like to use 90 days same as cash? Or, we can spread this out over 12 months to make it fit within your budget."

   _______% of the 90 days same as cash contracts convert to payments which are usually at _______% APR with a rule of 78's prepayment penalty.

   The ads that you see in the Sunday paper (those color slicks) are not free advertising. The company has to not only pay for the printing and the shipping of the ads, but it also costs them around $24,000 to have it inserted in the paper for one day. So they are paying around $25,000-$30,000 to have these put in the paper and are offering you "free money" with the 6 months same as cash. This may seem like a great deal, but in reality, the interest and cost of the advertising has already been included in the price of the item.

3. ______, radio, and other ___________

Repetition is paramount when it comes to advertising. The constant barrage of messages over and over sticks with consumers. Why else would companies spend millions to come up with catchy slogans?

8.1 Name 5 slogans and the product they represent.
1.
2.
3.
4.
5.

4. Product _______________

This is when companies utilize advertising and in-store product positioning to encourage consumers to respond to their products.

- **BRAND RECOGNITION** also known as **BRANDING** is a form of traditional (TV, Radio, Print) and nontraditional (bumper stickers, street poster) advertising aimed at creating consumer awareness for a specific trademark or distinctive name identifying a product or a manufacturer.
- **COLOR** is another aspect to pay attention to in advertising. Catching the consumer's eye is very important in marketing strategies. Some companies spend millions to find just the right color combination to grab the consumer's attention.
- **SHELF POSITIONING** is where research is done to find just the right place in the store to get consumers to purchase specific items. Why do you think milk and meat are in the back of grocery store? Perhaps it's to get you to pass a lot of items before you get back to them.
- **PACKAGING** an item to look more appealing is another strategy utilized to promote and sell products.

Significant Purchases

A "Significant Purchase" is normally an item over $_________.

The body goes through physiological _________ when making a "Significant Purchase".

You have to be careful with big-ticket items. Many times you will experience something known as "buyer's remorse". This is when you wake up the next morning and ask yourself, "what have I done?"

Carefully considering large purchases prior to making the purchase is a great way to guard against buyer's remorse.

8.2 Name a "Significant Purchase" you have made and tell if you had "buyer's remorse."

What To Do When Considering A "Significant Purchase"

Because you can always spend more than you ________ you must develop a POWER OVER ____________.

One definition of maturity is learning to delay pleasure!

These 5 Steps Will Help You In "Significant Purchase" Decision Making:

1. **Wait ____________________ before making a purchase.**

   Research and study the item you are considering to purchase. Give yourself a chance to calm down and get over the "fever" of wanting the item.

2. **Carefully consider your buying __________.**

   Is this a "need" or a "want"? Your basic needs are food, shelter, clothing, transportation, and utilities. Everything else is basically a "want."

8.3 Name 3 of your needs and 3 of your wants. Explain why they are needs and wants.
Needs:
1.
2.
3.
Wants:
1.
2.
3.

No amount of _________ equals contentment or fulfillment.

"For where your treasure is, there your heart will be also."
Matthew 6:21 (The Bible, NKJV)

Enjoy life and remember: you can buy **fun**, but **happiness** has to come from within!

3. **Never buy anything you do not fully ______________.**
   Especially when it comes to investments, insurance, and real estate!

4. **Consider the "Opportunity _______" of your money.**
   If your money is one place it can't be in another.

   Let's say you have $10,000 to spend. Well, you could buy a $10,000 car but you would have nothing left to invest. If you invested it all, you could not buy the car. Look at what would be best in regards to spending the money. Money is finite. It has a beginning and an end.

5. **Seek wise _________.**
   If you are married, consult your spouse. If you are single, go to someone you trust and respect.

Money in Review 8

Vocabulary

Define the following terms:

APR	**Finite**	**Opportunity Cost**
Buyer's Remorse	**GNP**	**Rule of 78's**
Financing	**Impulse Purchase**	**Significant Purchase**

True/False

Determine whether these statements are true or false. If false, change the bold word to make it true.

1. ___ Good salesmen answer a question **with a question**. _______________
2. ___ Shelf positioning is done to cause **impulse purchasing**. _______________
3. ___ Advertising slicks cost about **$2,000** to run in one Sunday paper. __________
4. ___ To consider your buying motives means asking yourself **if you can afford something**. _______________________
5. ___ Never buy anything you **do not fully understand**. _____________________

Completion

Complete the following statements:

1. ______% of 90 days same as cash convert to payments.
2. A "significant purchase" is anything over $________.
3. You must develop a power over _____________.
4. No amount of __________ equals contentment or fulfillment.
5. You should always consider the _____________ cost of your money.

Matching

Match the term with the best statement:

____ 1. Seek the counsel of your ________.

____ 2. You need to wait ____________ before making a major purchase.

____ 3. Most 90 days same as cash contracts convert to payments at _______% interest.

____ 4. Borrowing money and paying over time is called __________.

____ 5. The average person will view over _________ advertisements a day.

A. 24
B. Financing
C. 78
D. Spouse
E. 4,000
F. Overnight
G. Lender
H. 6,000

Multiple Choice

Choose the best answer for the following questions:

1. Which of the following is not a category in Product Positioning?

A. Color B. Packaging C. Price D. Shelf Positioning

2. Companies must have ___________ to survive.

A. Managers B. Products C. Sales D. Employees

3. The __________ society is advertised to more than any other in the world.

A. American B. European C. Canadian D. African

4. Companies choosing certain shelf positions is an example of:

A. Picky owners B. Advertising C. Selective shopping D. Product Positioning

5. By asking yourself, "Why am I buying this product?", you are examining your:

A. Necessities B. Checkbook C. Buying motives D. Conscience

Discussion

1. Have you ever fallen for financing as a marketing tool? How?
2. Have you ever purchased something and then felt guilty afterward? Explain.
3. How does advertising affect your buying decisions?
4. What is the biggest "impulse purchase" you have ever made? Why did you purchase the item?
5. If you owned a business, how would you market your product?

Case Studies

Read the following case studies and write down what you would tell these individuals, if you were their financial advisor.

1. Bret and Emily are looking to buy a new couch and the one they want is $999. They only have $200 saved, but they can get it 6 months same as cash. They figure they could buy the couch and save up the extra $799 over the 6 months and save the interest by paying it off early. Is this a good idea? What would you do?
2. Sherry is looking to buy a car but only has an extra $275 per month in her budget. She has found a dealer that will lease her a very nice car for $225 per month over 4 years. She is very excited because not only is she getting a nice car, but she is also saving $50 per month in payments. What could be better? What would you say to Sherry if she asked for your opinion?

Watch Your Step

Rearrange the letters into their appropriate column to reveal a message. Letters can only be used with in the column directly above them.

*Spaces containing punctuation marks do not require a letter.

	B		S					O		D			N				S	
	H	O	T	U	R		F	E	O	L		O	H			A	N	
D	E	U	O	E	E		R	O	U	S	E	S	O	E	M	O	H	F
C	N	V	T	H	A	S	F	O	O	L	I	H	R	F	H	A	I	L
I	W	I	I	C	E	A	H	A	L	S	T	A	E	D	S	T	O	E

chapter 9

understanding insurance

Objectives:

At the completion of this chapter, you should be able to:

- Explain why insurance is an essential part of a healthy financial plan
- List the different types of insurance coverage
- Compare Term and Cash Value Life Insurance

Key Terms:

Deductible
Liability
Replacement Cost
MSA
Elimination Period
Term Insurance
Self-insured

Pocket Change

Strange Insurance

- **Alien Abduction Insurance**
  Cost: $150 per year for $1.5 million coverage
  Note: One claim has been paid
- **Pet Insurance**
  Cost: $171 per year with a $40 deductible
  Note: Older pets require a higher premium
- **Werewolf Insurance**
  Cost: $150 per year for $1.5 million coverage
  Note: Pays only if you turn into one
- **Wedding Insurance**
  Cost: $125 per year for $3,000 of cancellation coverage
  Note: Doesn't cover last-minute breakups
- **Wine-Collection Insurance**
  Cost: 50 cents to $1 per $100 of value
  Note: Covers theft, breakage, and other unsavory situations

Source: Kiplinger's

Say the word insurance, and watch people run for cover. It's a great way to clear a room at a party. Few other subjects engender the same feelings of confusion, frustration, and all-out distaste—not that it's hard to understand why. Stiff competition in the industry has given rise to more options and price ranges. The same policies can vary by hundreds of dollars, depending on the company. And if you don't know what you're looking for, you can buy more coverage than you need and miss out on significant discounts.

As tempting as it can be to give in to the confusion and avoid buying insurance at all, insurance provides an important hedge against the risk of loss of income or property by transferring the risk to an outside source. So when those things that "will never happen to you" happen, someone else helps foot the bill and you don't wind up declaring bankruptcy.

Although there are entire books on the subject of insurance, we will examine the six basic kinds of insurance, what they protect, and how much you need:

- Homeowners or Renters Insurance
- Auto Insurance
- Health Insurance
- Disability Insurance
- Long-term Care Insurance
- Life Insurance

According to the Bankruptcy Institute, more than 50 percent of consumers go broke because of medical bills. What would have happened if those consumers had had adequate insurance in place to cover their bills? It is financial suicide not to have health and disability insurance. If you have a family, I will go so far as to say it is irresponsible not to have health and disability insurance, unless you are prohibited from obtaining it. It is very expensive; as a matter of fact, it is often robbery. But then, you can lose a lifetime of work by not having it. You should carefully investigate and understand the options so that you know what your coverages are and then shop around.

Despite what the insurance agents out there may tell you, you can have too much insurance. And you pay too much for it for you to be an insurance ostrich—that is, someone whose head is in the sand.

Don't be overwhelmed by the sheer complexity of unusual types of insurance. Remember the KISS principle I use for investing: Keep It Simple, Stupid! Keep your insurance premiums low and continue to save in your emergency fund. You will be ready for life's unexpected events.

Insurance is something most people do not want to talk about until the time comes that they need it. However, insurance is one of the most important parts of a healthy financial plan. You should have several different types of coverage in place. Insurance can quickly become expensive, but it is well worth it! Without it, all your financial planning could come tumbling to the ground!

Insurance can be very complicated, so it is a good idea to understand how it works. When you decide to speak with an insurance agent, make sure they explain all of the details so you fully understand them, otherwise seek out another agent!

The purpose of insurance is to ___________ risk.
Without proper coverage, an accident or loss could bankrupt you!

Unless you have a large amount of cash, you need to transfer that ____________ to someone who can afford to pay it!

Types of Insurance you should have:

1. ______________________________
2. ______________________________
3. ______________________________
4. ______________________________
5. ______________________________
6. ______________________________

Saving Money On Insurance

Homeowner's And Auto Insurance

There are ways to save money as far as insurance premiums are concerned.

1. **You can raise your ______________.**

   Raising your deductible from $250 or $500 to $1,000 will save money on your monthly premiums. If you have a fully funded emergency fund in place, you should be able to do this. You will be taking on an additional financial risk, so it is a good idea to do a "break-even-analysis." This will enable you to determine if the savings in premiums justifies the added risk.

   For example: If you change your deductible on your auto insurance from $250 to $1,000, you are taking $750 more risk.

   - If this saves you $30 per year in premiums, you divide the $30 into the $750 to give you 25. This means you will have to go 25 years without an accident or claim to "break even".

   - If it saves you $250 per year in savings, then the "break even" would be only 3 years.

2. **Always carry adequate ____________.**

This is one of the best buys on the market. It does not cost much money at all to raise your liability from $250,000 to $500,000. You should carry at least $500,000 in liability coverage both on your home and your auto. Liability coverage insures you if something is your fault.

3. **With your older cars you may consider dropping your ____________.**
If you choose to drop your collision, you need to make sure you have enough money to buy a replacement car for cash.

9.1 Research the difference between the following areas of auto insurance:
1. Liability
2. Collision
3. Comprehensive

9.2 Using the Internet, compare the cost of insurance rates for various automobiles.

Check your Homeowner's Policy for the following:

4. **With your homeowner's insurance, you need ____________________ cost.**

In reference to "Replacement Cost", if your home were completely destroyed by fire, the insurance company will "replace" it regardless of its value. Stay away from the dollar amount coverage; your home may appreciate to an amount that is greater than your coverage. If this happens, you will lose the difference. You want things to be replaced. That was why you purchased insurance in the first place.

5. **An ____________ policy is a big liability policy that is an umbrella over the top of your auto and homeowner's insurance.**
It is not very expensive to get several million dollars in coverage over your existing liability policies. When you start acquiring larger assets (i.e., house, car, furniture), you will need to consider this type of coverage. For only a few hundred dollars a year you can really protect yourself and your family. You have worked hard for your possessions…protect them.

Health Insurance

To save money on your health insurance, increase your ____________________.

Health insurance is extremely expensive, but you must have it! Depending on which statistics you look at, credit cards and medical expenses are #1 and #2 when it comes to personal bankruptcy filings.

Raising your co-insurance amount is a good way of saving money. The co-pay or co-insurance is often referred to as "80/20". After you have paid the deductible, the insurance company will pay 80% and you will pay 20%. If you change your co-pay to a 70/30, you are taking on more risk, but your premiums will go down. Again, with a fully funded emergency fund, you can afford to do this.

Deductible Tip:
Deductibles start over each year. For example, if you have a $250 deductible and paid the entire amount this year, you will be starting over again at the beginning of next year with a fresh $250 deductible.

You can also increase your ________-loss.

Stop-loss is your maximum out-of-pocket expenses after both the deductible and co-pay have been paid. For example, if you have a $5,000 stop-loss, once your out-of-pocket expenses, including both the deductible and co-pay have reached $5,000, the insurance company will now pay 100%.

For self-employed people, you may consider the ________.
This is a Medical Savings Account, also known as the Medical IRA.

This is a major medical insurance policy with a very _________ deductible.

With the MSA, there is a tax-deductible savings account attached. This will save you a tremendous amount of money in premiums. Your deductible, however, will be a lot higher. You can save, tax-deductible, up to 75% of your deductible into a savings account every year.

For Example: Your old premium was $450 per month, but with the MSA, your new premium is only $150 per month, a savings of $300 per month. If your deductible is $4,500 per year, you can save $3,375 into a tax-deductible account. It grows tax deferred and you can use it for medical care with no penalties and no taxes. If you do not use it, it is still your money...not the insurance companies.

Term Tip:
Maximum Pay is the amount that insurance companies will pay over one's lifetime before they stop coverage. You should always keep your "maximum pay" at one million dollars or more.

Disability Insurance

This is probably the most overlooked type of insurance!

Disability insurance is to replace __________________ lost due to a short term or permanent disability.
Statistics show that you are 12 times more likely to become disabled than you are to die before the age of 65, if you are currently 32 years of age.

Buy disability insurance that pays if you are unable to perform the job you were educated or __________ to do.

This is called _______________ disability.

9.3 List some careers that people are educated to do that would fall into this category. Why would this type of coverage be so important?

The availability of disability insurance has a lot to do with the type of work one does. For example, a construction worker would have a more difficult time getting disability coverage than would a teacher. The more hazardous the job, the harder it is to get coverage and also the expense is greater.

Buy long-term coverage...to age 65 or for ________.

Beware of ________-term policies.

9.4 How can you guard against short-term disabilities? For instance, a 3 or 6 month disability?

Your coverage should be for about ______% of your take-home pay.

Many disability policies cover only 50% of your take-home pay. Some policies may pay up to 70%, so investigate thoroughly!

The ________________ period is the deductible in a disability policy.

This is the time between being declared disabled and when the payments begin. A 90-day elimination period is average. If you have 6 months of expenses in an emergency fund, you could have a 180-day elimination period, thereby lowering your premiums. As your savings grow, you can lengthen your elimination period.

The ____________ the elimination period, the ___________ your premium cost should be.

Long-Term Care Insurance

Long-term care insurance is for ___________ home or in-home care.

This should be considered for people 60 years of age or older. Statistics say that the largest expense facing the baby boomer is elder care. We feel a responsibility to take care of our parents. It is important to discuss this with parents or look into it yourself if you are 60 years old or older.

_____% of people over the age of 65 will take on some type of elder care and _____% of these will need it for 5 years or longer.

The expense of not planning for long-term care could be catastrophic to your financial situation.

Life Insurance

The purpose of life insurance is to replace lost income due to __________.

So in reality, it is __________ insurance.

The problem with life insurance is that most people have no ______ what they _______.

Basically, there are 2 types of life insurance:

The first is _________ insurance that is for a specified amount of time or term...thus the name.

Term insurance is renewable in 5, 10, 20, and even 30-year increments. Your age and time of renewal can increase the premium price.

The second type is called _______________ insurance. It is much more expensive than term and it has a savings account built in.

Most policies in this country are "cash value". Statistics show that almost 75% of the policies sold are "cash value".

The myth about life insurance is that it is a ______________ situation and is ever growing.

If you are saving and investing over time, you can become what is known as self-___________________.

Let's Do the Math:

Self-Insured
With planning, becoming self-insured is not that difficult...for example:

- Let's imagine that Joe is 30 years old and his wife is 29. They have two children, ages 6 and 3. They have a mortgage and other expenses associated with two children. In this situation, if Joe suddenly dies, his wife would be in big trouble without life insurance.

- Let's turn the clock forward 20 years. Joe is 50 and his wife is 49. The two children are 26 and 23. With a 15-year mortgage the house is now paid for and the children are on their own. After saving for 20 years, there is approximately $750,000 dollars in investments. If Joe died at age 50 with the planning that he and his wife had done...she would be fine. They are now self-insured.

Cash-Value Life Insurance
Understand that "Cash-Value" life insurance is very expensive, for example:

- A 30-year old male can purchase $125,000 in coverage, for $100 per month. Within this policy, cash value savings begins to build up. By the time he is 60 years old, the cash value has grown to $41,000 and all along he has had $125,000 in coverage. This sounds like a good deal on the surface...insurance and savings all in one. However, you could get the same $125,000 in term insurance for about $7 per month! So you have spent an extra $93 per month to build that cash value. Had you invested that same $93 per month in good growth stock mutual funds, you would not have $41,000 in value, but $327,000!

  Looking at the example above, not only is he not saving with cash-value insurance the way he would with term, but he is also under-insured. With the average income in America being $40,000, the $125,000 in coverage would not last long and here's why. You need to have approximately ten times your income in coverage to protect your loved ones. Ten times $40,000 means he needs $400,000 in coverage. If his wife invests the $400,000 at 10%, she could take $40,000 per year in interest from the account, thus replacing his income. With only $125,000 in coverage, she could only pull off $12,500 at 10%. In the end, she would be forced to drastically change her lifestyle.

- Cash-value insurance is also called "Whole Life". Similar policies out there that build up cash value are called "Universal" and/or "Variable" life insurance.

- The other horrible thing about cash-value other than the so-called "savings plan" is that if you die, your beneficiary gets the face value of the policy, but any savings you had built up, goes directly to the insurance company.

Term Life Insurance
The best insurance bargain.

- Let's look at the new numbers. A $400,000 term policy would cost about $20 per month. Then save the other $80 that was going to the cash-value policy. Invested in good mutual funds, this should grow to about $279,000 by age 60. Still a far cry from the $41,000 the cash-value insurance was giving him.

- Go with 20-year level term, guaranteed renewable, and stay away from cash-value policies.

One more time...TERM!

Do not invest with life insurance. You wouldn't take your car with a bad transmission to a muffler repair shop, would you?

Even a non-income earning spouse should have coverage to replace what they do, and an at-home spouse does a lot that has a tremendous economic impact on the family!

In cash-value insurance, the returns are historically ________.

When you die with cash-value, the insurance company ________ the cash value you had been building up.

Also, the ________ are extremely ________.

What To Buy:

Buy only low cost, level __________.

Do not forget your __________.

Stay away from the fancy __________.

Children only need enough for __________.

Remember: you need about 10 times your income on you!

Insurance To Avoid

Avoid _________ life and ____________ disability.
This will pay a loan off if you die. With proper life insurance coverage, why would you need this?

Do not get credit ________ protection.
Better yet, do not get a credit card and this will not be an issue!

You do not need ____________ insurance.
Major medical will cover this!

Do not get accidental _________ insurance.

Any _________ value or refund feature.

Do not buy pre-paid __________ policies.

Do not buy mortgage __________ insurance.

Stay away from ________________ coverage.

Money in Review 9

Vocabulary

Define the following terms:

Auto Insurance
Bankrupt
Beneficiary
Break-even Analysis
Cash Value Insurance
Catastrophic
Claim
Co-insurance
Collision
Comprehensive
Contents Policy
Co-pay
Coverage
Credit Disability
Credit Life
Deductible
Elimination Period
Guaranteed Renewable
Health Insurance
Homeowners Insurance
Level Term
Liability
Life Insurance
Long Term Care Insurance
Long Term Coverage
Maximum Pay
Mortgage
Mortgage Life
MSA
Occupational Disability
Out-of-Pocket
Permanent Disability
Policy
Premiums
Renters Insurance
Replacement Cost
Self-insured
Short-term Disability
Short-term Policy
Stop-Loss
Take-home Pay
Tax-deductible
Term Insurance
Umbrella
Universal Life
Variable Life
Whole Life Insurance

True/False

Determine whether these statements are true or false. If false, change the bold word to make it true.

1. ___ Mortgage life insurance is a **good** buy. ____________
2. ___ Cash value life insurance is a **good** way to save money. __________
3. ___ With a level term life insurance policy, the premium **stays the same** over the life of the policy. _______
4. ___ Term life insurance is **less** expensive than whole life insurance. _________
5. ___ Children only need enough life insurance to cover the cost of **college**. _____________
6. ___ The purpose of insurance is to **transfer** risk of a loss to a company that can afford to pay it. ________
7. ___ The **stop-loss** is what you pay before insurance will begin paying. ____________
8. ___ With older cars you may consider dropping your **liability**. ____________
9. ___ Buy **Long Term Care** insurance that covers you to age 65 or for life. ___________
10. ___ A stay at home mom **does not need** life insurance coverage. __________

Completion

Complete the following statements:

1. A __________ is what you pay monthly to keep an insurance policy up-to-date.
2. An ___________ policy provides additional liability.
3. ______________ is the 80/20 with a Health Insurance policy.
4. ______________ ______________ pays you if you are unable to perform the job you were educated or trained to do.
5. The amount of life insurance coverage you should have is ______ times your income.

Matching

Match the term with the best statement:

____ 1. This insurance covers income lost due to death.	**A.** Term
____ 2. This type of insurance covers damage to a vehicle.	**B.** MSA
____ 3. This type of insurance has a savings plan built in.	**C.** Whole Life
____ 4. You should get this type of insurance when you turn 60.	**D.** Life
____ 5. A major medical policy with a high deductible for self-employed people.	**E.** Long-Term Care
	F. Auto
	G. ESA

Multiple Choice

Choose the best answer for the following questions:

1. **If you cause a car wreck, the portion of the policy that pays for your car is called:**
   A. Collision B. Health C. Comprehensive D. Term
2. **Life insurance that is payable only if the insured dies within a specified period of time is called:**
   A. Cash Value B. Variable C. Term D. Universal
3. **A term insurance premium that remains unchanged throughout the life of the policy is called:**
   A. Unchangeable B. Level C. Variable D. Fixed
4. **The time between when one is disabled and payments begin is:**
   A. One month B. Elimination Period C. Deductible D. 3-6 Months
5. **Which of the following is not a type of cash value insurance:**
   A. Whole Life B. Variable Life C. Term Life D. Universal Life

Discussion

1. Explain two ways you can save money on auto insurance.
2. Why should you get a "contents policy" if you live in a dorm?
3. Explain why life insurance should not be used as a savings plan.
4. Discuss what is meant by "buy term and invest the difference".
5. Why do you think most people do not purchase disability insurance?

Case Studies

Read the following case studies and write down what you would tell these individuals, if you were their financial advisor.

1. Sonya's brother sold her a $100,000 whole life insurance policy and she is paying $125 per month in premiums. She is single and has since found out that term insurance would be a better buy. She wants to change but is afraid she will hurt her brother's feelings by doing so. What would you tell Sonya to do in this case?
2. Bill and Anne have two young children, ages 2 and 4, and they are not currently covered under any life insurance policy. Anne is a full-time mom and brings in zero income. Bill currently makes around $45,000 per year in income. They are just barely able to make their monthly payments on all of their stuff, so getting life insurance coverage does not seem like a pressing issue at this time. What would you suggest Bill and Anne do when it comes to life insurance coverage?

Insuring Your Future

E	I	M	U	A	U	N	Y	X	P	E	O	F	U	Z
L	N	G	I	Y	B	T	A	S	I	C	X	L	R	J
B	S	L	U	A	G	D	K	U	C	I	Y	G	V	P
I	U	P	A	A	L	T	P	U	R	K	N	A	B	D
T	R	O	T	S	R	C	P	I	Q	Y	X	T	I	D
C	A	L	Y	Y	R	A	I	C	I	F	E	N	E	B
U	N	I	B	T	T	E	N	D	F	F	M	E	C	A
D	C	C	V	I	I	P	V	T	X	P	R	N	O	L
E	E	Y	O	C	M	L	R	I	E	H	E	A	L	L
D	T	N	W	O	E	K	I	E	N	E	T	M	L	E
P	A	H	T	L	A	E	H	B	M	U	D	R	I	R
L	S	Y	Y	T	I	L	I	B	A	I	L	E	S	B
H	O	M	E	O	W	N	E	R	S	S	U	P	I	M
R	E	N	E	W	A	B	L	E	L	O	I	M	O	U
C	O	V	E	R	A	G	E	V	R	D	Z	D	N	F

BANKRUPT
COLLISION
DISABILITY
HOMEOWNERS
OCCUPATIONAL
PREMIUM
UMBRELLA
BENEFICIARY
COVERAGE
GUARANTEED
INSURANCE
PERMANENT
RENEWABLE
UNIVERSAL
CLAIM
DEDUCTIBLE
HEALTH
LIABILITY
POLICY
TERM

unit 4

real estate and mortgages

careers and extra jobs

collections and credit bureaus

chapter 10

real estate and mortgages

Objectives:

At the completion of this chapter, you should be able to:

- Explain the things you should do when selling a home
- Explain the things you should do when buying a home
- Explain the benefit of a 15-year mortgage as opposed to a 30-year mortgage
- List the 5 types of home loans

Key Terms:

Curb Appeal
Realtor
MLS
Inflation Hedge
Appraisal
Conventional Loan
Loan to Value
Principal

Pocket Change

- The median new home price in the 1960's was $20,000 as compared with the 1990's median new home price of $133,000.
- In 1999, Florida led the nation with the percentage of home sales that were paid with cash (20%), Kansas was at the bottom with 10%.
- Your house payment should not exceed 25% of your monthly take-home pay.

Home Facts

- In 1999, 13.3% of homes were purchased with cash.
- Median value of primary residence: $100,000
- Median home equity: $38,000
- Americans who own a second home: 12.8%
- Median monthly mortgage payment: $720
- New mortgages with adjustable rates: 19%

Source: 1999 -Kiplinger's/Acxiom/DataQuick

"When are you going to buy? You're throwing your money down a rat hole by renting".

Aside from the appeal of having your own backyard where the 2.5 kids can play with their shaggy dog while you and your spouse grill burgers and have "quality time", residential real estate is a great investment. In fact, the appreciating value of a house makes buying one a key to building long-term wealth. Except for parts of California and the Rust Belt, most of the country has watched residential real estate double and triple in value over the past twenty-five years. As a result, houses have created a hedge against inflation.

In addition to being a great investment, your personal residence became an even more important investment with the advent of the 1997 tax-law changes. Now couples can sell their personal home every two years and make a tax-free profit of up to $500,000 (singles up to $250,000). Wow! This is yet another reason to have home ownership in your long-term plans. What's more, it allows some of you who want or need to move to a less expensive house and become debt free to do so without a tax penalty.

Just because a house is a great investment, though, doesn't mean it's time to buy—nor does it mean you should buy the "dream" house you want to retire in. Two of the most common first-time buyer mistakes are buying too soon and buying more than you can afford, and so becoming house poor.

As you consider whether now is the time to buy a house, consider the following things:

- You may move in the next five years.
- Your life is in a state of flux.
- You have been married less than a year.
- You have not saved at least a 10 percent down payment on the house.
- You have to dip into the emergency fund for the down payment and closing costs.
- You still have debt.

Don't even think about venturing into home ownership if any of the above statements apply to you. Instead, take time to set some goals that will help get you ready to buy. (Example: Save $20,000 for a down payment by cutting back on entertainment and working extra). Create a realistic time line in which you can accomplish these goals.

You may not like it in the short run, but in the long run, you will be better off living by the Financial Peace rule of real estate: Less is best—less mortgage, less time paying off the loan (fifteen years or less, to be exact), and lower interest rates.

The "American Dream" Or The "American Nightmare"?

Mistakes with Real Estate can be a cost with zeros at the end.

Selling A Home:

When selling a home, you have to think like a ___________.

This is now a model home…your kids have to realize that they no longer live there. This is a product that you want in pristine condition and little handprints all over the place can cost you big bucks. The pets may need to take a vacation as well.

Clean up the house…and do not give a paint or carpet allowance. Do the painting and put down new carpet yourself. The home should be in near perfect condition.

The return on investment fix-up dollars is ____________.

New paint, wallpaper and some lawn care can help a home sell faster and for more money. If you were looking at two comparable homes and one was cleaned up and trimmed perfectly but the other one was not…which one would you choose? A little elbow grease will save you time on the market and could make you thousands of dollars more at the time of sale.

The most important aspect of preparation is attention to what is known as ___________ appeal.

Give attention to detail. Go out and stand in the street, look at the house and say, "What needs to be fixed?" 60% of homebuyers become interested because they saw a "For Sale" sign in the yard. If the home needs work from looking at it, chances are the prospective buyers will keep driving. Make them want to look at the house. It needs to be enticing!

When prospective buyers walk up to your door they will look at the sidewalk to see if it is trimmed and they will stand on your front porch and look around. Get rid of the cobwebs and make sure the front door has a fresh coat of paint. Little things like this can and will help in the selling of your home.

The best Realtors are worth ________ than they cost, unless you are a seasoned pro.

Realtors help your home sell faster and help you from making costly mistakes. They have access to things that you do not…for example the MLS.

Exposure through the ___________ Listing Service is worth it.

You want to make sure that your Realtor is in the MLS because they will be able to expose your home to hundreds if not thousands of people…and that is what you want as a seller.

The MLS is a program that, if you are a buyer and you are looking for a particular type of home, will give you direction in where to find that home. Let's say you are looking for a home on two acres, has 4 bedrooms, 2 baths, and in a particular school system…this information is entered in to the MLS and results come out matching the criteria that was entered. The MLS speeds up the buying and selling process.

When selecting a Realtor, do _______ rely on friendships or relatives.

This is one of the largest assets you will ever sell. Interview and then hire a professional to do the work.

You should ___________ at least 3 Realtors.

You are hiring someone to do a job for you. Since you are paying around a 6% commission, the sale of a $100,000 home will cost you about $6,000 in commission. If you are going to pay that much money, you need to check references and the track record of the Realtor. You need to be choosy and find an agent that has sold millions of dollars in real estate per year.

Offering a home warranty typically will _______ make a sale...if the buyer asks for a warranty then consider it with that offer.

10.1 Name some other things that you should consider when selling a home:

Buying A Home:

Home ownership is a great investment for 3 main reasons:

Your mortgage is your house payment, which contains two components:

- the interest
- the principle.

1. **It is a __________ savings plan.**

   As you make your payments, a portion of the payment is going toward the principal, thus building up equity. Equity is your ownership portion, or what you could pocket if you sold the home. It is the investment part of your home, thus as a homeowner, you are building savings automatically.

2. **It is an __________ hedge.**

   This helps you keep up with inflation. A big part of inflation is home ownership. So, if inflation is running 7%, your home is keeping up with it.

3. **It grows virtually tax-_______.**

   If you have owned a home for at least 2 years, you can sell that home and make up to a $250,000 profit on it tax-free if you are single. If you are married filing jointly, you can make up to a $500,000 profit tax-free! Talk about a great deal!

Title Insurance insures you against an ________ title, which is when your proper ownership is in question. It is a good buy.

This is an insurance policy that states that you are the true owner. You always want to get Title Insurance.

Always get a Land Survey if buying more than a standard subdivision ________.

A land survey defines the boundaries of your property.
You wouldn't want to build a fence on your neighbor's property.

Realtor's access to the ________ system can make house hunting easier, BUT they think like a retailer.

Realtors can speed up the buying process, but when you are buying and using a realtor, try to find one that does not think "retail". You want to get one that is out to help you find a deal so you can ultimately save money.

What You Need To Buy:

You want to buy in the bottom price range of the ________________.

This gives your property more room to go up in value. If you buy a home that is in the top of the neighborhood, you have basically put a cap on the value of your home. Let's say you are in a $100,000 neighborhood and you add on to your home to bring the value to $130,000. People looking to buy $130,000 homes will not look in a $100,000 neighborhood...they are looking in $150,000 neighborhoods. You have limited yourself when it comes to selling. Always give yourself some flexibility when it comes to home appreciation!

Homes appreciate in good neighborhoods and are priced based on three things: ____________, ____________, and ____________.

Where a home is located generally dictates the price! Many times a small home in a good part of town will bring more than a larger home in a bad area of town.

If possible, buy near ________ or with a ________.

Homes near water sometimes bring as much as twice what similar sized homes away from the water will bring. It is the perception of seeing a duck land on the water that seems to drive people into buying lakefront property. So, if you can get a deal on a home near the water, this will ultimately mean more money at the time you choose to sell.

Buy bargains by overlooking bad landscaping, ugly carpet, ugly wallpaper, and the ________ print in the master bedroom.

Always buy a home that is (or can be) attractive from the ________ or has a good basic ________ plan.

You have to have an imagination when it comes to things that CAN be changed. Do not let the carpet color keep you from saving $10,000 when buying a home. You can change the carpet and you can paint the walls.

Things like a bad floor plan cannot be fixed unless you have saved so much money that you can afford to go in and structurally change the house. **Look for the bargains.**

Have the home inspected mechanically and structurally by a certified ___________ ________________.

A home inspector will check for any flaws such as bad wiring or plumbing. They are well worth the few hundred dollars you will pay for them. Check with the seller to see if they will pay for a home inspector. Many times they will, if it will speed up the sale of the home.

Appraisals are an "__________ of value", but a better opinion than the seller's. Order an appraisal if in doubt about value.

Many times the seller has emotion and sentiment tied up in a home. Therefore it is a good idea to get an outside party to determine a value.

Mortgages:

First, remember to _______ debt.

The best way to buy is the ______% down plan.

Many people are unwilling to do this because they are in a hurry to get into a home. It may seem strange to rent for a while in order to save up and pay cash for a house. Imagine never having a house payment. Your friends will think you are weird...but you will be a wealthy weirdo!

`Live like no one else, and eventually you will live like no one else!`

If you must have a mortgage, try something different, like putting 50% down and paying it off in 7 or fewer years.

Your house payment should be for no more than ______% of your take-home pay.

Typically, you can qualify for almost twice the amount. However, if you spend that much, you will be what is known as "house poor" and run the risk of having very little money left over to save for repairs, car replacement, retirement, or college funds. You always want to have the flexibility to save money for expenses that come along...never tie up all of your money in one thing!

Get no more than a _______ year mortgage with at least a _____% down payment and an emergency fund left over after closing.

In 1929, only 2% of the people in the USA had a mortgage. By 1962, only 2% did not have a mortgage. Maybe our patience is diminishing a little bit.

Look at the difference in a 15 vs. a 30-year mortgage at 8% interest:

Loan Amount	Years	Monthly Payment
$95,000	15	$907 mo.
$95,000	30	$697 mo.
		Difference of $210 mo.

The balanced owed:
15 year = $44,000 30 Year = $83,000

30 Year Mortgage News:

- After 10 years you have paid $83,600 in payments but you have only paid down $12,000 in principal.
- 98% of your payments in the first 2 years go directly to interest.

The Adjustable Rate Mortgage (ARM's) were brought on with the advent of ________ interest rates in the early 1980's.

The concept of the ARM is to ______________ the risk of higher interest rates to the ___________ and in return the lender gives a lower rate at the beginning.

The question is, why would you get an ARM when interest rates are low anyway? You are starting on the floor and the only way the rates are likely to go is up. If you have an ARM, refinance to a fixed 15-year mortgage or less.

According to the FDIC more than _______% of ARM's are adjusted inaccurately, so if you have one check it.
You can qualify for a larger house with ARM's, but the risk of financial stress later is not worth it.

Ways To Finance A Home:

1. **The ____________________ loan, usually through the FNMA and insured against default privately.**

   Down payments range from 5% to 20% or more and these loans are available in all forms and formats.

   With 20% down or a 20% LTV (Loan to Value), you can avoid PMI which is ____________ Mortgage Insurance.

   Private mortgage insurance is Foreclosure Insurance that protects the mortgage holder in the event of a foreclosure. They are insured so that they do not lose money on your loan. This will run some where around $70 per $100,000 borrowed per month so once you reach 20% equity you will want to have this dropped.

2. **The _________ loan, which is insured by HUD-The Federal Government.**
   FHA stands for Federal Housing Administration.

   The down payments can be as low as _____% and are used on lower priced homes.

   These loans are currently _________ expensive than conventional financing so you should avoid them.

   They are not a good deal for the consumer.

3. **The ______ loan, which is insured by the Veteran's Administration.**

   These are designed to benefit the Veteran. The seller is responsible for paying everything--appraisal, closing costs, etc., allowing a true zero-down purchase for the Veteran. The point is, however, to avoid debt...putting nothing down is not wise.

   With a good down payment the conventional loan is a ___________ deal.

4. **___________ financing is when you pay the owner over time making him the mortgage holder.**

This is a _________ way to finance because you can be creative in the structure of the loan.

With Owner Financing you can set up terms any way you want. For example: no payments for a year or early payoff incentives.

The Assumption Loan is where you pay the owner their equity and then take over the payments. These are not as common as they used to be.

Real Estate Recommendations:

- **Go with a CONVENTIONAL LOAN**
- **No more than a 15 year FIXED rate**
- **20% down payment**
- **Better yet, save up and PAY CASH**
- **Live the AMERICAN DREAM**

Money in Review 10

Vocabulary

Define the following terms:

Appraisal
Appreciation
ARM
Assumption Loan
Conventional Loan
Curb Appeal
FDIC
FHA Loan
Fixed Rate
Floor Plan
Home Inspector
Home Warranty
House Poor
Inflation Hedge
Land Survey
LTV
MLS
Owner Financing
PMI
Principal
Realtor
Retailer
Title Insurance
VA Loan

True/False

Determine whether these statements are true or false. If false, change the bold word to make it true.

1. ___ The ARM began in the **1960's**. _______
2. ___ **Appraisals** are opinions of value. ___________
3. ___ You want to buy in the **middle** price range of the neighborhood. _________
4. ___ The return on investment that fix-up dollars represent is **minimal** when selling a home. ___________
5. ___ The **Conventional** loan is insured against default through the FNMA. _________

Completion

Complete the following statements:

1. The most important aspect of preparation is attention to what is known as _________ appeal.
2. You should always interview at least _____ realtors.
3. Always get a _______ __________ if buying more than the standard subdivision lot.
4. You should never get more than a ______-year mortgage.
5. You can avoid Private Mortgage Insurance with a _______% down payment.

Matching

Match the term with the best statement:

____ 1. This type of loan is where you pay the owner their equity and then take over the payments.

____ 2. With this type of loan, you can make a true zero-down purchase.

____ 3. This type of loan allows for a lot of flexibility with the terms.

____ 4. These loans are typically more expensive and are insured by the Federal Government.

____ 5. This is the recommended type of loan you should get. Down payments range from 5-20% or more.

A. Conventional
B. VA
C. Assumption
D. Owner Financing
E. ARM
F. FHA

Multiple Choice

Choose the best answer for the following questions:

1. **This is foreclosure insurance on your home.**

   A. PMI   B. ARM   C. SEPP   D. LTV

2. **Which of the following is NOT a reason Home Ownership can be a great investment?**

   A. Forced savings plan   C. Grows virtually tax-free
   B. Inflation Hedge   D. Zero interest financing

3. **This is the recommended type of financing you should get when buying a home:**

   A. VA   B. FHA   C. Assumption   D. Conventional

4. **When buying, you need to overlook:**

   A. Floor Plan   B. Curb Appeal   C. Wallpaper   D. Price

5. **If your home is worth $200,000, you can drop PMI if you owe ___________.**

   A. $160,000   B. $170,000   C. $180,000   D. $190,000

Discussion

1. Explain ways you could save up enough to buy your home with cash.
2. Why would you want to keep your house payment less than 25% of you monthly take-home pay?
3. What are the advantages of having a fully funded emergency fund before you buy a home?
4. Why do people want to get into a home as quickly as possible and what are some ways to avoid buying too soon?
5. Why would a 30-year mortgage have a higher interest rate than a 15-year mortgage on the same loan amount?

Case Studies

Read the following case studies and write down what you would tell these individuals, if you were their financial advisor.

1. Justyna and Derrick are engaged to be married in three months. They have found a home they wish to purchase. They have the option to get a conventional or a VA loan. With the conventional loan, they will have to put 5% down. With the VA loan, they can move in with a zero-down purchase. They have enough money to pay the down payment on the conventional, but they want to have some money to buy furnishings and other items they may need. Derrick is a veteran, so the VA looks very attractive. What would you suggest for them?

2. Jerry and Pam are looking into an Adjustable Rate Mortgage as a financing option. They have found a house that they want to buy, but they will barely be able to make the payments on a fixed interest rate. With the ARM, they are sure they can make the payments. By the time the rates increase, they are expecting to have pay increases at their work. At that time they figure they may change to a fixed rate. They are going to go with a 30-year mortgage, and they will pay extra whenever bonuses come in. They are tired of renting and love this house. What would you advise Jerry and Pam to do?

Mortgage Mania

Unscramble each of the clue words. Then, reveal the hidden message, by copying the letters in the numbered cells to the empty spaces at the bottom of the page.

Clue												
SARPAPLAI	☐	☐	☐	☐ 11	☐	☐	☐	☐	☐			
ETRILERA	☐	☐	☐	☐	☐	☐	☐ 5	☐				
ARLOETR	☐	☐	☐	☐	☐	☐ 12	☐					
CIAPEAPERT	☐	☐	☐	☐	☐ 15	☐	☐	☐	☐	☐		
NEVNACTOOLIN	☐	☐	☐	☐	☐	☐	☐	☐ 2	☐	☐	☐	☐
CETSIPNOR	☐	☐ 7	☐ 17	☐	☐	☐	☐	☐	☐			
LAFNINTOI	☐	☐	☐	☐ 14	☐	☐	☐	☐	☐			
WRTAANYR	☐	☐	☐	☐	☐	☐	☐	☐ 8				
NERWO	☐	☐	☐	☐ 9	☐							
SYREVU	☐ 16	☐	☐ 13	☐	☐	☐						
RAGTOGEM	☐	☐	☐	☐	☐	☐ 10	☐	☐				
CNNAFNIIG	☐ 1	☐	☐	☐	☐	☐	☐	☐	☐			
BALDASJEUT	☐	☐	☐	☐	☐	☐ 4	☐	☐	☐	☐		
TAER	☐	☐	☐	☐ 6								
FIDXE	☐ 3	☐	☐	☐	☐							

☐	☐	☐	☐	☐	☐	☐		☐	☐	☐	☐	☐	☐	☐		☐	☐	☐	☐
1	2	3	4	5	6	7		8	9	10	11		12	13		14	15	16	17

chapter 11

careers and extra jobs

Objectives:

At the completion of this chapter, you should be able to:

- Explain the difference between a Vocation, a Career, and a Job
- Explain a resumes' purpose
- List the 3 things you should do when targeting potential employment opportunities
- List 4 reasons to get a part-time job or work over-time

Key Terms:

Vocation

Career

Job

Resume

Lump Sum Savings

Pocket Change

- In the 1960's, 37% of women worked in the workplace as opposed to 57% today.
- U.S. surveys estimate that as many as 67% of workers dislike their jobs.
- According to the June 6, 2001 issue of *U.S. News and World Report*, nearly 40% of U.S. workers are experiencing so much stress over financial worries that their productivity suffers.
- According to a recent Gallop Poll, 55% of today's employees have no enthusiasm for their work.

I Do Not Choose To Be A Common Man

It is my right to be uncommon — If I can.

I seek opportunity — not security. I do not wish to be a kept citizen, humbled and dulled by having the state look after me.

I want to take the calculated risk; to dream and to build, to fail and to succeed.

I refuse to barter incentive for a dole. I prefer the challenges of life to the guaranteed existence; the thrill of fulfillment to the stale calm of utopia.

I will not trade freedom for beneficence nor my dignity for a handout. I will never cower before any master nor bend to any threat.

It is my heritage to stand erect, proud and unafraid; to think and act for myself, enjoy the benefit of my creations and to face the world boldly and say, This I have done.

By Dean Alfange

All this is what it means to be an American.

The career or type of work you choose—and whether or not you choose to work at it—can be paramount to your financial peace. Viktor Frankl, author of *Man's Search for Peace*, says, "Life is never made unbearable by circumstances, but only by lack of meaning and purpose". Thomas Edison said, "The secret of success is focus of purpose".

We will spend well in excess of 100,000 hours of our lives working at our choice of vocation. The sheer math of a per-hour rate makes this decision very important. You must plan your work and then work your plan. Happy and effective people have found a vocation for which they have a natural aptitude and have committed themselves to excellence in that vocation.

Everyone has some natural talent or aptitude in one or more areas. If you can identify those areas you not only will be happier and perform more successfully in that role, but you will also become better paid for that. Our free-market system pays for performance at some point. When you have a natural talent or aptitude, coupled with desire and experience, the result is productivity plus.

If you are good at something, you become more intense, and so you get more creative. Consequently, you accomplish more, so you get paid more. This causes you to enjoy it more, which in turn means you will get better at it. This process is what we call the excellence cycle. If you get caught up in an excellence cycle, you will find that your financial problems will no longer be caused by a low income.

When you find the right field of endeavor for you, you will excel financially only if you work hard and are honest. The same light widely disbursed in a room simply lights the room, but when focused to the size of a pin it becomes a laser. At this point you must do some self-inspection to determine if you are lazy. That may seem to be a strange suggestion, but I have never met a lazy person who thinks he is lazy.

If you take time off and call it a sick day when you are not sick or if you work half-speed when the supervisor is not watching, you are guilty of theft. You steal from the company that supports your family, but worst of all, you steal from yourself and make a statement about who you really are.

It is time we turned the corner on this issue of low productivity. Sadly, in most cases, low productivity results when people simply do not work hard. In managing people, or being managed, we must maximize our time. To "be all you can be" eventually results in a pay-raise.

Forty percent of Americans have not read a nonfiction book since their last day of formal education. It's time to turn off the television and put down the romance novels and improve your intellect so you can increase your earning power.

Careers And Extra Jobs

With financial planning, it is important to have something you do that has meaning in your life to bring in income.

> If your outgo exceeds your income, eventually
> your upkeep will be your downfall!
>
> - Anonymous

You should manage what you have better. You should live on less than you make. But sometimes you just need more money.

The average job in America only lasts for _______ years.

You need to be ready to change at all times because change is a way of life. Most people have a misconception that the majority of businesses are large in structure. However, nearly 80% of the businesses in this country have fewer than 10 employees.

Business Employment Trends

0-4 employees	59.3%
5-9 employees	19.2%
10-19 employees	11.6%
20-49 employees	6.6%
50-99 employees	2.0%
100-499 employees	1.42%
500-999 employees	0.28%

Small businesses drive America.

11.1 Name 3 small businesses in your area and explain the impact that they have.

1.
2.
3.

The average person will have between _____ - _____ jobs or positions over their lifetime.

The days of working for a company for 40 years, retiring with a gold watch and a pension are just about gone. Very seldom will you find this type of company in today's society. You have got to be willing to change. Not doing so can mean staying in a very stressful position.

Look at it this way, if you lose your job, maybe it was time for you to go out and do what you were put on this earth to do. In what most would consider a major negative setback, look at it as a positive thing and be excited about the opportunity that lies ahead. Your fully funded emergency fund provides flexibility. Having a "financial umbrella" means that you won't have to take the first job that comes along.

Studies tell us that about _______% of college graduates are working in something totally unrelated to what they got their degree in.

Not only do jobs and careers change, but it's also important to remember that people change. What you think you want to do with your life will change as time passes. Your priorities change and what you think will make you happy will change. As you grow and take on more responsibility, such as with a spouse, children, a home, and of course the monthly expenses of living, you begin to see things through a different set of glasses.

Experts tell us that _______% of the products and services we are now using will be obsolete in 5 years.

Back in the 1920's and 1930's before refrigeration came about, ice would be delivered to homes for the iceboxes. These iceboxes kept things cool. When the advancement of refrigeration was born, the ice companies could have panicked, but instead they just crushed the ice and put it in plastic bags to sell. They just "changed" their way of doing things to stay in business. That is what you have to do…you have to change with the times or you will be left behind.

11.2 List 5 things that have changed since you were born:
1.
2.
3.
4.
5.

The key to having power in our careers is to first look at ____________________.
Be yourself, accept yourself, and know what you want out of life. Do not do anything just because your family did it!

___________ should not be the core issue when it comes to the job motivation.

Many people associate money with happiness. Money is necessary to pay expenses, save, and invest, but if you are not happy in your work, ultimately the money will not matter as much. Your stress level will rise and you will not look at things the way you should. If you do something well and with passion, money will eventually follow.

With a job there must be a sense of _____________, a sense of _____________, and a sense of _____________________________.

Just because you have the ___________ to do something does not mean that it's what you should do with your life.

"Life is never made unbearable by circumstances, but only by lack of meaning and purpose."
- Viktor Frankl

You should pick a career that blends your ________________, your ________________, your ______________________________, your ____________________, your ____________________, your ______________________ and your ______________________.

If any of the above is lacking when it comes to your job, you should rethink what you are doing. For instance, if everything is in place except you are not "passionate" about the work, maybe you need to do something that you are passionate about.

11.3 Give an example of how a lack of "passion" can affect your work performance.

Your _______ is not your life...it is simply one tool for a successful life.

Don't put too much stock in things that could change, as they probably will. Put your priorities in order. Remember, you need to "play" sometimes...don't take life so seriously!

Your ________________ is a "calling".

This is what you feel you were meant to do with your life. This can be great thing. Your vocation is something you love; you are on "vacation" for the rest of your life!

A _____________ is your line of work...not your "calling".

Too many people have a ________.
70% of Americans literally hate their job. For them, their job has become a daily activity to produce an income.

You have the choice to change. Even if it takes a little time, you need to strive toward the point that you absolutely love getting up every morning to go to work.

The major quest in life is not what you ___________ ___________________, but what you ___________ ___________________.

11.4 Discuss a job that would pay you a lot of money, but that you would hate to do.

Understanding your ____________ style will tell you more about where you will function successfully than knowing your ____________________ background.

Education is important, but it is your personality that lends itself more to success. Your drive and determination will lead you to prosperity. Follow your passion…you are here for a purpose…you will discover it and when you do, move in that direction!

A recent Harvard University study reported that _______% of the reason for a person's success is due to technical skill and knowledge, while ______% of the reason for success originates from the person's personal skill, their attitude, their enthusiasm, their self-discipline, and their ambition.

SET GOALS!

"Show me a stock clerk with goals and I'll show you a CEO. Show me a person without goals, and I'll show you a stock clerk"

- J. C. Penney

The reason that candidates with the best ________________ on paper seldom get the job is because employers are looking for personality and team players that fit within their organization.
A fabulous resume does not guarantee employment.

Resumes do not get you jobs. They get you ____________.

You are selling "you"…and you know yourself better than anyone…be proud of who you are and be confident in your abilities and it will show.

Most hiring decisions are made in the first _________ minutes of an interview.

11.5 What does the above statement say about the interview process and about the person conducting the interview? What can you learn from that?

Ads in the newspaper only represent about _______% of what is available.

11.6 Other than newspapers, list some sources for finding employment.

When targeting possible employment opportunities, you should do the following 3 things:

1. **Send out an ________________________**
   Let them know you will be contacting them...don't be arrogant about it, but this is sort of a "heads-up" to the prospective employer that you are on your way.

2. **You will then send them a ____________ _____________ along with a __________.**
   At this point, let them know what experience you have and how it applies to the position that you are seeking. Convince them that they need you as much as you need them.

3. **Tell them also you will be giving them a ___________ _______________.**
   One of the key ingredients to success is persistence. Not to the point that you are a pest, but the whole idea is to show that you are a determined person who wants to reach their dreams and goals.

Taking an active approach with the above 3 steps for __________ days will help you land a job.

There are situations where you do not need a career, but a supplemental income for one reason or another.

Many times the best way to meet short-term _____________ is to take the dreaded ___________ - __________ job.

Here are some examples of short-term objectives:

1. **To eliminate ___________ bills.**
   These are the little bills that just hang around and drive you crazy.

2. **_________ _________ debt.**
   This will help you get rid of those credit cards, car payments, school loans, and who knows what else?

3. **To ___________ an item with cash.**
   If you have been longing for a new a car or that much needed vacation...try this approach instead of the heavily marketed bank loan.

4. **To build up ________ sum savings.**
   This is ideal when you would like to set aside some extra money to save, invest for retirement, or invest for the kids college fund.

Home-based businesses are another way to supplement income. Currently about 45% of American homes have a business within its walls. These are called "Cottage Industries". These are fun to have and can be profitable.

> "Do not overwork to be rich; Because of your own understanding, cease! (5) Will you set your eyes on that which is not? For riches certainly make themselves wings; They fly away like an eagle toward heaven."
>
> – Proverbs 23:4-5 (The Bible, NKJV)

Beware to not allow your work (career) to be the source of all your satisfaction and self _______________.

"Think beyond your lifetime if you want to accomplish something truly worthwhile."

- Walt Disney

Some ideas of successful home-based businesses are:

Accounting	Wedding Planning	Personal Service	Senior Citizen Care
Appliance Repair	Graphic Design	Gift Baskets	Newsletters
Vending	Delivery Service	Interior Decorating	Flea Market Vendor
Landscape Design	Home Inspection	Window Displaying	Ceiling Fans
House Painting	Auto Detailing	Glass Tinting	Power Washing
Catering	Nutrition Counselor	DJ Service	Jewelry Sales
Tree Removal	Chimney Cleaning	Glass Etching	Firewood Supply
Kitchen Tune-ups	Decks & Coverings	Mail Order	Balloon Vendor
Pet Sitter	Real Estate Photos	Aerial Photos	Books
Computer Consultant	Web Designer	Marketing	How-To-Brochures
Sewing Alterations	Tour Guide		

Personal Mission Statement Worksheet

Skills and Interests: ______________________________

____

____

Personality Traits: ______________________________

____

____

Values, Dreams, and Passions: ______________________________

____

____

MY MISSION IS: ______________________________

____

____

"Outstanding people have one thing in common: an absolute sense of mission."

-Anonymous

Examples Of A Mission Statement

I will maintain a positive attitude and a sense of humor in everything I do. I want to be known by my family as a caring and loving husband and father; by my business associates as a fair and honest person; and my friends as someone they can count on to earn their respect. Controlling all my actions is a strong sense of integrity, which I believe is the most important character trait.

My Mission is to provide service, products, and benefits with integrity and honesty to the medical community. I will look for opportunities to help hurting individuals and assist other professionals in a win-win manner. I will not knowingly harm or take advantage of anyone. I will use my knowledge and abilities in organizing and structuring in ways that provide income and pleasure for my family and blessings to those around me.

My Mission is to exercise my creativity and innovative ideas by developing songs, books and products, which change lives and society for the better. I will use my talents and abilities consistently. I will not hide them simply because they will not always be immediately recognized. I want all of my work to be a product of God's inspiration and a blessing to the world. I will be loyal to my family, friends and God.

For myself, I want to develop self-knowledge, self-love, and self-allowing. I want to use my healing talents to keep hope alive and express my vision courageously in work and action. In my family, I want to build healthy, loving relationships in which we let each other become our best selves. At work, I want to establish a fault-free, self-perpetuating, learning environment. In the world, I want to nurture the development of all life forms, in harmony with the laws of nature.

Personality Inventory

Instructions:

In each box, circle each word or phrase that describes a consistent character trait of yours. You should find groupings in 1 or 2 categories. Then turn to the next page for corresponding career areas.

Dominance (Driver)

Likes Authority
Takes Charge
Controlling
Bold
Decision Maker
Enterprising
Task Oriented
Overlooks Detail
Not careful of other's Feelings
Adventurous
Determined
Self-reliant
Independent
Confident
Very Direct

Influencing (Expressive)

Enthusiastic
Visionary
Takes Risks
Spontaneous
Enjoys Change
Group Oriented
Likes Variety
Creative New Ideas
Optimistic
Infectious Laughter
Inspirational
Initiator
Promoter
Can Waste Time
Entertains Others

Steadiness (Amiable)

Calm
Loyal
Nurturing
Dry Humor
Sympathetic
Conscientious
Peace Maker
Enjoys Routine
Understanding
Avoids Conflict
Dislikes Change
Maintains Low Profile
Can Be Slow to Act
Good Listener
Reliable

Compliance (Analytical)

Predictable
Controlled
Perfectionist
Diplomatic
Inquisitive
Accurate
Orderly
Factual
Loves Detail
Conscientious
Reserved
Discerning
Precise
Scheduled
Sensitive

Occupational Categories

Instructions:

In the boxes below are some of the occupations that line up with the personal characteristics you checked on the previous page. These are broad categories, but will give you an idea of what would be most fitting for you. This is not a complete list, but will give you an idea of how types of jobs use the same personal skills.

Dominance

Manufacturer's Representative
Lobbyist
Business Manager
Fire Marshall
Travel Guide
Principal
Fashion Coordinator
Landscape Architect
Sales Agent, Insurance
Production Coordinator
Show Host/Hostess
Manager, Customer Services
Sales Agent, Real Estate
Announcer
Writer
Entrepreneur
Business Owner

Influencing

Training Representative
Clergy Member
Manager, Advertising
Editor
Preschool Teacher
Arbitrator
Sales Agent
Administrator, Health Care
Home Economist
Actor/Actress
Reporter
Manager, Office
Insurance Sales
Optometrist
Illustrator
Faculty Member
Interior Design

Steadiness

Investigator
Pharmacist
Physical Instructor
Psychologist
Survey Worker
Counselor
Social Worker
Teacher, Secondary School
Correspondence Clerk
Market Research Analyst
Veterinarian
Nurse
Podiatrist
Programmer
Lab Technician
Chiropractor
Librarian

Compliance

Medical Record Technician
Nurse, Licensed Practical
Nurse, General Duty
Secretary
Accountant
Job Analyst
Mail Clerk
Caseworker
Architect
Biochemist
District Ext. Service Agent
Geologist
Physical Assistant
Historian
Environmental Analyst
Airplane Pilot
Painter

Money in Review 11

Vocabulary

Define the following terms:

Ambition	**Cover Letter**	**Obsolete**
Career	**Job**	**Part-time Job**
Contact Letter	**Lump Sum Savings**	**Resume**
Cottage Industries	**Objectives**	**Vocation**

True/False

Determine whether these statements are true or false. If false, change the bold word to make it true.

1. ___ Home-based businesses are also called **"cottage industries"**. _______________
2. ___ Your **vocation** is your "calling". ___________
3. ___ One reason to get a part-time job is to **get out of the house**. _____________
4. ___ Money **should be** the primary issue when it comes to motivation with a job. _________
5. ___ Conducting an active job search strategy should land you a job within **5-7** days. _______

Completion

Complete the following statements:

1. The average job in America lasts for only _______ years.
2. The key to having power in our careers is to first look at ____________.
3. Your "____________" is a calling.
4. _______% of Americans literally hate their job.
5. Resumes do not get you jobs, they get you ______________.

Matching

Match the term with the best statement:

____ 1. A _________ is your line of work.
____ 2. Just because you have the _______ to do something does not mean it is what you should do with your life.
____ 3. ______% of the businesses in this country have fewer than 10 employees.
____ 4. A ______ is just an activity to bring in income.
____ 5. Ads in the newspaper represent only ______% of the available jobs.

A. Vocation
B. 80
C. Job
D. 15
E. Ability
F. Desire
G. Career
H. 25

Multiple Choice

Choose the best answer for the following questions:

1. **Any job you have must blend all BUT which of the following:**

   A. Skills B. Obligation C. Abilities D. Personality Traits

2. **The average person will have ________ jobs in their lifetime.**

   A. 16-18 B. 5-7 C. 10-12 D. 18-25

3. **______% of American homes have a small business within their walls.**

   A. 33 B. 65 C. 50 D. 45

4. **Experts tell us that ______% of all products and services we are now using will be obsolete in 5 years.**

   A. 75 B. 80 C. 85 D. 90

5. **A _____ is a daily activity that produces income.**

   A. Job B. Career C. Vocation D. Goal

Discussion

1. Do you know anyone who hates their job? Why do you think they continue doing it?
2. What strategies do you have in getting a job?
3. If you are going to further your education, how do you think that will benefit you when looking for a job?
4. How will you value income when it compares to satisfaction with a job?
5. Would you do something you did not like in order to make five to ten times more than the average worker? Why or why not?

Case Studies

Read the following case studies and write down what you would tell these individuals, if you were their financial advisor.

1. Sheila is a nurse, and she is not happy with her situation even though her income is above average. She wants to go back to school to get a degree to teach, but she realizes it will cost money to go to school. Her income as a teacher will be about half of what she is used to making. She is torn between being unhappy in a good paying job or making a sacrifice when it comes to income to be happy. What should Sheila do?

2. Ryan loves his work but is making only enough for him and his wife to get by. They have no savings put aside, and they have $5,000 in credit card debt. His income is only $27,000 per year, but now he has been offered a position making $65,000 per year. He is considering taking the job even though he knows he will eventually hate what he is doing. He figures he needs to make as much as possible for his family, as his wife is expecting their first child. What advice would you give Ryan?

Make Your Vocation Your Vacation

Similar to the TV game show, Wheel of Fortune, fill in the blanks to reveal a message. Letters appear in random order, there is no "code."

A	B	C	D	E	F	G	H	I	J	K	L	M	N	O	P	Q	R	S	T	U	V	W	X	Y	Z
				5													8								

__ __ __ E   __ __   __ E __ E R   __ __ __ E
17 21 4 5   21 10   7 5 11 5 8   18 12 20 5

__ __ __ E __ R __ __ __ E   __ __
23 7 1 5 12 8 12 1 17 5   1 26

__ __ R __ __ __ __ __ __ __ __ E __
9 21 8 9 23 18 10 24 12 7 9 5 10

__ __ __   __ __ __ __   __ __   __ __ __ __   __ __
1 23 24   15 7 17 26   1 26   17 12 9 2   15 4

__ E __ __ __ __ __   __ __ __   __ __ R __ __ __ E
18 5 12 7 21 7 14   12 7 20   19 23 8 19 15 10 5

chapter 12

collections and credit bureaus

Objectives:

At the completion of this chapter, you should be able to:

- Explain how to handle aggressive collectors
- Define Credit Bureau and Credit Report
- Explain how you can handle credit report corrections yourself

Key Terms:

Garnishee

Disposable Income

Credit Bureau

Bankruptcy

Credit Report

Forms:

The following useful forms can be found in the appendix.

- Credit Bureau Info sheet page 172
- Sample Removal Letter page 173
- Sample Credit History Report page 178
- Request for File Disclosure Form page 174
- Sample Cease & Desist Letter page 175
- Sample Credit Bureau Letter page 176
- Sample Creditor Letter page 177

Pocket Change

- 10% of bankruptcy filers were delinquent only 5 to 29 days before bankruptcy.
- Bankruptcy losses make up about 3% of lender's outstanding debt.

Over The Edge

- The following is a list of topics that put debtors "over the edge" to actually filing bankruptcy. Collection tactics include repossession, wage garnishment, foreclosure and collector harassment.
  - Litigation: 5%
  - Taxes: 6%
  - Divorce: 7%
  - Other: 10%
  - Medical: 11%
  - Unemployment: 12%
  - Collection Tactics: 49%

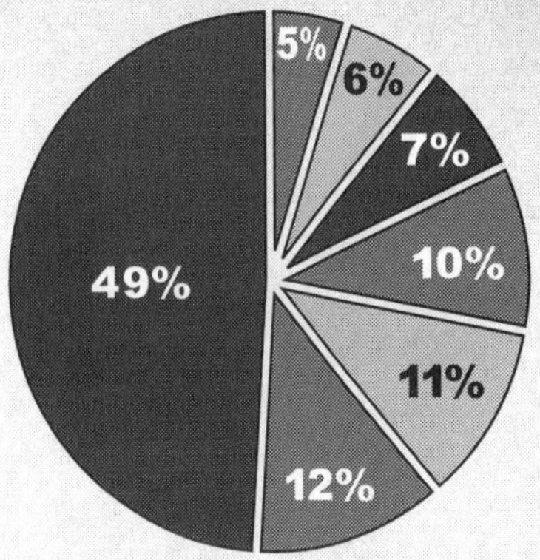

Source: VISA U.S.A. INC.

What is one of the dumbest plants you can think of? My vote goes to the cucumber—round, green, and good for very little except to make the perfect pickle if picked before maturity. The other two subjects we are to discuss in this chapter are also to be picked before maturity. If you let them die on the vine, without stunting their growth, you will wish you hadn't. Cucumbers if let go can at least be used on a salad, but if you let a credit report problem or collector go, they will spoil your whole dinner with indigestion.

Remember in "Dumping Debt", we decided borrowing money was not the way to go, so you may be wondering why you need a clean credit record. First, many potential employers pull a credit report as an indication of character, thus a job hunt could be harmed by an unclean report. Second, even when you do not borrow for cars, credit cards, or any consumer goods, many will go for a five- or ten-year mortgage to get your home and get debt free quickly. So many people who have a goal of being debt free want a clean report for a short-term mortgage.

Under no circumstances should you get one of those high-fee rip-off secured credit cards to "build your credit". All this does is confirm for the mortgage company that you have not learned your lesson. As a matter of fact, if you have several open credit card accounts with zero balances, most mortgage lenders will count that against you because the day after closing you could furnish your home at 18 percent interest. In the real world, you become bankable if you make all bad accounts right and then pay on time any open accounts, including rent, for one to two years. If you have bad credit or you are just starting out, do not borrow to create a good credit report.

We strongly recommend that you fix all credit report problems yourself. Do not hire one of these credit cleanup firms because you don't need it. There are some legitimate cleanup firms, but that industry abounds with scam artists, which is another reason to do it yourself. Please do not believe anyone who tells you that they can legally remove accurate information from your report. If you did what the report says, you'll have to live with it for a while, and if you don't believe me, you are setting yourself up for a disappointment and a con.

It is time for you to see a light at the end of the tunnel, one that is not an oncoming train. The best and the most honorable way out of debt is with a plan. You set your plan and your priorities, not your creditors; otherwise, they will drown you. The best way for them to get paid is for you to take control of your financial destiny. You and your spouse set your goals, work hard, work often, live on little, and get out so you never have to talk to people whose sole job is to "technique" you again. Don't get me wrong: people should pay their debts and there are legitimate collections firms who use reasonable procedures to collect unpaid accounts, but it is the abuses we see daily in our office that we want to help you walk through. Remember, hope cannot be taken from you; but, you can *choose* to surrender it.

Collection Practices

Debt is the most aggressively marketed product in our culture today.

The best way to pay off debts is with a _________.

Bankruptcy is not the answer. Most bankruptcies are for less than $20,000 and the people filing them are those that lose hope and give up. With a plan you can avoid this and take control of your finances.

A collector's job is not to help your overall situation; it is to get ________ money only.

They are trained ___________ ________________ or ___________________________.

They are typically low paid positions with a high ____________ rate.

They do not stay on the job long. The average time on the job is 92 days.

There are some good collectors out there, but they are usually confined to local agencies, mortgage companies, or small businesses in your area.

The reaction you give based on their collection tactics will be databased and used to encourage future payment.

They are taught to evoke strong ___________.

Their goal is to make you very afraid or very angry. That way you will **not** be thinking rationally. If you **are** thinking logically, you would take care of necessities first. Only when you are irrational would you pay the credit card bill before you keep the lights on in the house. Keep in mind, you **do** need to pay these people, but only after you have taken care of **your** priorities. Once your basic needs have been met, your stress level goes down and you will be better equipped to handle your other responsibilities.

The way you counter act this technique is to always pay necessities first and then _________ set the order of payment.

Your priorities should be: Food, Shelter, Clothing, Transportation, and Utilities. If you have these walls built up, you can take on just about anything. It is when you are stressed and worried that you are the most vulnerable and collectors know this.

In 1977, a consumer law was passed by congress called the **Federal Fair Debt Collection Practices Act** to protect you from unfair collectors. The law technically only applies to collection agencies (not your creditor), but later court cases make most creditors also abide by the FFDCPA.

The Act states that harassment is illegal. Collectors may only call between the hours of ________ and ________ (unless you've given them permission otherwise).

This is YOUR time so you may consider getting a "time/date" stamp on your answering machine if this gets to be a problem.

The Act also allows you to cause a creditor to cease calling you at ________.
You should request this in writing by certified mail return receipt requested.

Send your request certified mail, so you are able to show a proof of receipt that they received the letter.

The Act even allows you to cause a creditor to stop ALL contact ________ to notify you of lawsuit proceedings.

Do not use a cease and desist letter except in ________ situations because all negotiations stop and any hope of a positive resolution is lost.

Typically, you are better off to communicate with collectors. Send them more information and call them more often than they call you. This gives you more footing to stand on with collectors and may result in a negotiating atmosphere that is more friendly.

No collector or creditor may confiscate a ________ account or garnish ________ without proper and lengthy court action. So, all such threats are a bluff.
They have to sue, win, and then execute on the judgment before any of the above can take place.

12.1 How would you react to threats made to you by collectors? Do you know someone who has had to deal with overly-aggressive collectors? How did they deal with them?

Your plan should include as much prompt repayment as possible. Refrain from allowing collectors to set your priorities. YOU need to set the priorities. Do not let a collector use your credit report as a ________ club.

Most people can make their minimum payments. However, if you are having difficulty making minimum payments, use what is known as the ________ - ________ plan.

After you have paid your necessities, the money left over will be considered your "disposable income". Take the total amount you owe in debt and divide that into what you owe each creditor to determine the percentage each debtor will receive.

For example: If your total debt is $2,000 and you owe Discover $1,200...Discover makes up 60% of the total debt.

If your disposable income is $200, you take 60% of the $200, which would be $120 and pay Discover. That is their "fair share".

Item	Total Payoff	Total Debt	Percent	X Disposable Income	= New Payment
Discover	$ 1,200	$ 2,000	.6	$ 200	$120
CitiBank	$ 300	$ 2,000	.15	$ 200	$ 30
MBNA	$ 200	$ 2,000	.10	$ 200	$ 20
Sears	$ 200	$ 2,000	.10	$ 200	$ 20
Penney's	$ 100	$ 2,000	.05	$ 200	$ 10

Send the collectors a copy of your budget along with a letter explaining your situation, thus letting them know that you will be paying them what you can. They will complain and continue to call, but you have to stand firm and realize this will go on your credit report as a "gray" mark. A gray mark is when you have paid, but not on time. A black mark is when you have not paid at all. They may threaten to sue, but rarely will they if you are sending them something. Strangely enough, as much as they complain about the amount you are sending, they always seem to cash the checks.

Eventually, if you are making NO payments and have cut NO deals, you WILL get sued!

Typically lawsuits for under __________ are sued in General Sessions Court (small claims court). This is a fairly informal proceeding.

Before you are sued, you will be served by the local Sheriff's Department and given typically ______ days notice of the court date.

If the debt is valid, even if you fight, you will lose.

From that date you will have _________ days before the judgment becomes final and garnishments or attachments begin.

The number one catalyst to bankruptcy is collections pressure. Generally speaking, people have a hard time dealing with confrontation and will just throw up their hands and give up. Fight through the tough times!

At ANYTIME during the process you may settle with the creditor or the attorney IN WRITING. If you are not able to reach agreement you can file with the court a "______________ motion", also called a pauper's oath in some states.

Make sure you get anything you agree on with a creditor or attorney **IN WRITING, IN WRITING, AND IN WRITING**. Is that clear?

Credit Bureaus

All information is removed that is _____ years old except a Chapter 7 bankruptcy, which stays on ______ years.

This means from the last time the company you owe reports the debt, this information will stay on for 7 years. Each time it is reported, the 7 year clock starts over…so the information could be on there for much longer if it is reported often.

Beware of credit clean-up scams.

The only information that may be legally removed from a credit report is ____________ information.

Over _______% of the credit bureau reports have errors. So you should check your credit report at least every ____ to ____ years.

Another Act passed in 1977 is the Federal Fair Credit Reporting Act which deals with how credit bureaus, creditors, and consumers interact.

With identity theft on the rise in this technology based society and numbers floating everywhere, you really need to monitor your credit report, just in case someone is committing fraud against you.

The Act requires a credit bureau to remove all __________________________ within a "reasonable time" of notification of such inaccuracies.

"Reasonable time" has been defined by court cases as 30 days.

So, to clean your credit report of inaccurate information you should write a separate letter for each inaccuracy and staple a copy of your credit report to each letter circling the account in question. You should request that "inquiries" be removed also.

All of these letters should be sent via ____________ mail, return receipt requested to prove when they receive the letter and start the 30-day clock ticking.

If the credit bureau does not prove the accuracy of the account within 30 days, then you should request they remove the ________________ account from your file.
You will have to be assertive after the 30-day period!

The Federal Trade Commission and The State Consumer Affairs division is where ________________ should be lodged.

The moral is...Pay your bills! Don't let yourself be taken advantage of during the process of working through your plan. It's YOUR plan.

You can settle your debts with some companies if you offer them a lump sum. You should only do this if you do not have the full amount you owe them.

For example: If you owe a company $2,000 and all you have is $1,100...offer them the $1,100 and see if they take it. Make sure that if they take the offer you get it in writing. You want them to state in the letter that this is a "Settlement in Full".

Tax Tip:

Forgiven debt is a taxable event. Let's say you owe $5,000 and the company agrees to settle for $3,000. The other $2,000 is considered taxable income and you will receive a 1099 form at tax time.

The great thing is, if you never borrow money
you will never have to deal with collectors!

Facts You Should Know

- Payment history on your credit file is supplied by credit grantors with whom you have credit. This includes both open accounts and accounts that have already been closed.

- Payment in full does not remove your payment history. The length of time information remains on file is:
  - Credit and Collection accounts: 7 years from the date of last activity
  - Courthouse records: 7 years from the date filed, except bankruptcy Chapters 7 and 11 remain for 10 years from the date filed

- New York State Residents only: Satisfied judgments 5 years from the date filed; paid collections 5 years from the date of last activity with original creditor.

- A divorce decree does not supersede the original contract with the creditor and does not release you from legal responsibility on any accounts. You must contact each creditor individually and seek their legal binding release of your obligation. Only after that release can your credit history be updated accordingly.

- There may be apparently duplicate accounts reported in your credit file. This could occur because some credit grantors issue both revolving and installment accounts. Or, an account may appear twice twice because when you move, some credit grantors transfer your account to a different location and issue another account number.

- The balance reported is the balance on the date the source reported the information. Credit grantors supply information on a periodic basis, so the balance shown may not be the balance you know it is today. If the balance reported was correct as of the date reported, it is not necessary to reinvestigate the balance on that account.

- Many companies market consumer products and services by mail. Millions of people take advantage of these direct marketing opportunities because it is a convenient way to shop. If you prefer not to receive direct marketing mailings, you can write to: Direct Marketing Association, Mail Preference Service, P.O. Box 9008, Farmingdale, New York 11735-9008. Include your complete name, full address, Social Security number and signature. The Direct Marketing Association will have your name removed from these lists.

Money in Review 12

Vocabulary

Define the following terms:

Bankruptcy
Credit Bureau
Disposable Income
FFDCPA
Chapter 7 Bankruptcy
Credit Report
FFCRA
Garnishee

True/False

Determine whether these statements are true or false. If false, change the bold word to make it true.

1. ___ You should always pay the **collectors** first. _______________
2. ___ Any time you deal with **collectors** by mail, send it certified mail, return receipt requested. _______________
3. ___ Collectors are typically low paid, **low** turnover positions. _________
4. ___ Collectors are trained **tele-marketers**. ______________
5. ___ The best way to pay debts is with a **plan**. _________

Completion

Complete the following statements:

1. A collector's job is to get your ____________.
2. The Federal Fair Debt Collections Practices Act was passed in _________.
3. To give creditors their "fair share", use what is known as the ___________ plan.
4. Lawsuits for under ___________ are sued in General Sessions Court.
5. You should check your credit report every _____-_____ years.

Matching

Match the term with the best statement:

____ 1. A Chapter 7 bankruptcy stays on your credit report for _______ years.
____ 2. "Reasonable time" is defined by the courts as _____ days.
____ 3. The only information that can be removed from a credit report is _____________ information.
____ 4. No collector or creditor can confiscate a ___________ account without proper court action.
____ 5. The FFDCPA states that a collector cannot call you except between the hours of _____ a.m. and 9 p.m.

A. 8
B. Inaccurate
C. 9
D. 7
E. 30
F. Checking
G. Retirement
H. 10

Multiple Choice

Choose the best answer for the following questions:

1. **The average time on the job for a collector is _____ days.**

   A. 30 B. 92 C. 77 D. 54

2. **You should always pay your ________ first.**

   A. Necessities B. Credit cards C. Car payments D. Student loans

3. **Over _____% of the credit reports have errors on them.**

   A. 25 B. 40 C. 65 D. 50

4. **A "forgiven debt" is a ______ event.**

   A. Happy B. Unfinished C. Bad D. Taxable

5. **This Act was passed in 1977 to protect you from unfair collectors.**

   A. FDIC B. FICA C. FFDCPA D. FHA

Discussion

1. What is the best way for a creditor or collector to get paid?
2. Do you know anyone who has had a bad experience with a collector? Explain.
3. How will you make sure your credit report is accurate?
4. How would you handle a collector if you were late making your payments?
5. Explain how the "Pro-rata" Plan works.

Case Studies

Read the following case studies and write down what you would tell these individuals, if you were their financial advisor.

1. Barry and Connie are late making their payments, and collectors are beginning to call on a daily basis. They are threatening to sue over the credit card debt that amounts to $13,000. The couple's car is about to be repossessed because they haven't paid the payment in 3 months. They are both working and are considering part-time jobs to catch up. They have a 16-year old son that plays sports at his high school, so they would have to miss his games. The collectors are getting more and more abusive with every call. What would you suggest Barry and Connie do?

2. Steve has not paid his credit card bill for the last 4 months and has been avoiding the collectors when they call. He owes $4,000 and has the money to pay it. He is going to try to cut a deal with the collectors to find out if they will take $2,000 and leave him alone. What advice would you give to Steve?

No Collectors... No Problem!

M	E	Y	K	F	N	I	S	R	K	W	G	E	Y	C
I	L	C	F	G	F	M	O	P	R	A	L	T	C	E
N	C	T	Z	N	A	B	R	I	R	B	I	S	A	R
I	J	P	G	C	O	R	T	N	A	T	I	R	R	T
M	P	U	S	V	Y	I	I	N	N	N	O	O	U	I
U	R	R	M	U	N	S	O	E	R	I	Z	R	C	F
M	B	K	T	G	H	S	D	A	Z	E	D	R	C	I
Q	J	N	R	E	A	I	C	W	K	G	P	E	A	E
W	D	A	E	E	C	O	L	L	E	C	T	O	R	D
W	I	B	R	L	V	H	U	A	H	F	B	E	P	A
T	I	D	E	R	C	O	N	A	W	P	L	A	N	V
R	X	A	J	Q	O	L	N	I	E	S	E	H	S	E
T	N	E	M	Y	A	P	E	R	Q	R	U	O	P	R
E	M	O	T	I	O	N	Q	M	U	U	U	I	L	S
K	B	G	U	P	B	O	D	E	U	T	E	B	T	H

ACCURACY
CERTIFIED
EMOTION
IDENTITY
PLAN
REPO
TURNOVER

BANKRUPTCY
COLLECTOR
ERRORS
LAWSUIT
REASONABLE
SCAMS
WRITING

BUREAU
CREDIT
GARNISHEE
MINIMUM
REPAYMENT
TECHNIQUE

"The Baby Steps"

Step 1: $1000.00 in an Emergency Fund
($500.00 if income under 20k per year)

Step 2: Pay-off all debt utilizing the Debt Snowball
(everything except the house)

Step 3: 3-6 months expenses in savings

Step 4: Invest 15% of household income into
Roth IRA's and pre-tax retirement

Step 5: College Funding

Step 6: Pay-off home early

Step 7: Build Wealth! (Mutual Funds/ Real Estate)

financial management forms

Getting Started

Welcome to the wonderful world of "cash flow management." Filling out these few forms and following your new plan will change your financial future. The first time you fill out the forms it will be tough and will take a while. But each time you come back for another look, you'll get faster and the forms will become easier, so don't get discouraged.

The length and the amount of detail I am taking you through may seem overwhelming. However, I have found that if you don't have the detail as a track to run on you leave something out. Guess what that does? If you leave items out that you are actually spending, you will crash your plan and then you will have an excuse to quit, so just bear down and do all the forms completely, one time.

Start with the Student Cash Flow Plan (page 149) and then move on through the other forms.

After you have filled out the whole set once, you only need to fill out the Cash Flow Plan at the beginning of each month, which should take about 30 minutes. Update the entire pack once per year or when any large positive or negative financial event occurs (Aunt Ethel leaves you $10,000 in her will).

Once you have made it through this planning process the first time, you should be able to manage your finances in 30 minutes per month plus what it takes to write checks and balance your checkbook. Go for it!

Monthly Retirement Planning

In order to retire with some security you must aim at something. Too many people use the READY-FIRE-AIM approach to retirement planning. Your assignment is to determine how much per month you should be saving at 12% interest in order to retire at 65 years old with what you need.

If we are saving at 12% and inflation is at 4%, then we are moving ahead of inflation at a net of 8% per year. If you invest your nest egg at retirement at 12% and want to break even with 4% inflation you will be living on 8% income.

Step One:

Annual Income (today) you wish to retire on: **$30,000**

divide by **.08**

(nest egg needed) equals: **$375,000**

Step Two:

To achieve that nest egg, you will save at 12% netting 8% after inflation. So, we will target that nest egg using 8%.

$375,000	X	**.000436**	=	**$163.50**
Nest Egg Needed		Factor		Monthly Savings Needed

8% Factors (select the one that matches your age)

Age	Years to Save	Factor
25	40	.000286
30	35	.000436
35	30	.000671
40	25	.001051
45	20	.001698
50	15	.002890
55	10	.005466
60	5	.013610

Note: Be sure to try one or two examples if you wait 5 or 10 years to start.

Monthly Retirement Planning

In order to retire with some security you must aim at something. Too many people use the READY-FIRE-AIM approach to retirement planning. Your assignment is to determine how much per month you should be saving at 12% interest in order to retire at 65 years old with what you need.

If we are saving at 12% and inflation is at 4%, then we are moving ahead of inflation at a net of 8% per year. If you invest your nest egg at retirement at 12% and want to break even with 4% inflation you will be living on 8% income.

Step One:

Annual Income (today) you wish to retire on: ________

divide by **.08**

(nest egg needed) equals: __________

Step Two:

To achieve that nest egg, you will save at 12% netting 8% after inflation. So, we will target that nest egg using 8%.

_______________ **X** __________ = ____________________

Nest Egg Needed | Factor | Monthly Savings Needed

8% Factors (select the one that matches your age)

Age	Years to Save	Factor
25	40	.000286
30	35	.000436
35	30	.000671
40	25	.001051
45	20	.001698
50	15	.002890
55	10	.005466
60	5	.013610

Note: Be sure to try one or two examples if you wait 5 or 10 years to start.

Major Components of a Healthy Financial Plan

	Action Needed	Action Date
Written Cash Flow Plan	______________	__________
Will and/or Estate Plan	______________	__________
Debt Reduction Plan	______________	__________
Tax Reduction Plan	______________	__________
Emergency Funding	______________	__________
Retirement Funding	______________	__________
College Funding	______________	__________
Charitable Giving	______________	__________
Teach My Children	______________	__________
Life Insurance	______________	__________
Health Insurance	______________	__________
Disability Insurance	______________	__________
Auto Insurance	______________	__________
Homeowners Insurance	______________	__________

I (We), ______________________________________, a responsible adult, do hereby promise to take the above stated actions by the above stated dates to financially secure the well-being of my family and myself.

Signed:__________________________ Date:________________
(nerd)

Signed:__________________________ Date:________________
(free spirit)

How To Balance Your Checkbook

Keep your checkbook register current by subtracting both checks and withdrawals and adding deposits, as they're made, to keep your checkbook balanced correctly.

Balance your checkbook within 72 hours of receiving your bank statement (to make sure there aren't any mistakes).

What do I need in order to balance my checkbook?

1. Your Checkbook Register
2. Your Last Bank Statement
3. A Reconciliation Sheet (located on the back of most statements)

Where do I start? Checkbook vs. Bank Statement

Start by putting check marks, in your checkbook, for each of the checks and deposits included in your bank statement. Make an entry in your checkbook for any bank Service Charges (or interest paid) made by the bank.

Checkbook Register

Check Number	Date	Fee	Transaction Description	Payment	Deposit	Balance **$564.46**
5671	8/12	x	One Stop Grocery	57.40		507.06
5672	8/14		Electric Company	101.00		406.06
	8/14		Pay Check		700.00	1106.06
5673	8/16		Telephone Company	50.00		1056.06
5674	8/19		One Stop Grocery	66.00		990.06
		x	Bank Service Charge	2.50		**987.56**

Bank Balance Example

On the Reconciliation sheet, list any checks and/or withdrawals or other deductions that are in your checkbook that are not on your bank statement and total the list.

On the Reconciliation sheet, list any deposits that are in your checkbook but are not included on your bank statement and total the list.

Beginning with the ending balance from your bank statement, subtract the total withdrawals and add the total deposits that were not on your statement.

Compare with your checkbook balance. If they don't agree, double check your lists and re-add your checkbook entries until you find the difference.

List the balance from your bank statement $ 504.56

List the checks from your checkbook that aren't on your statement

The Electric Company	5672	8/14	101.00
Telephone Company	5673	8/16	50.00
One Stop Grocery	5674	8/19	66.00

TOTAL $ **217.00** (-) $ 217.00

List the deposit amounts in your checkbook that aren't on your statement

Pay Check	8/14		700.00

TOTAL $ **700.00** (+) $ 700.00

This should be your checkbook balance **$ 987.56**

Income Sources Worksheet

SOURCE	AMOUNT	PERIOD / DESCRIBE
Salary 1	$1,700	1st & 15th - $850
Salary 2	$1,300	2 WEEKS - $650
Salary 3		
Bonus		
Self-Employment		
Interest Income		
Dividend Income		
Royalty Income		
Rents		
Notes		
Alimony		
Child Support		
AFDC		
Unemployment		
Social Security		
Pension		
Annuity		
Disability Income		
Cash Gifts		
Trust Fund		
Other ________		
Other ________		
Other ________		
TOTAL	**$3,000**	

Income Sources Worksheet

SOURCE	AMOUNT	PERIOD / DESCRIBE
Salary 1	________	______________
Salary 2	________	______________
Salary 3	________	______________
Bonus	________	______________
Self-Employment	________	______________
Interest Income	________	______________
Dividend Income	________	______________
Royalty Income	________	______________
Rents	________	______________
Notes	________	______________
Alimony	________	______________
Child Support	________	______________
AFDC	________	______________
Unemployment	________	______________
Social Security	________	______________
Pension	________	______________
Annuity	________	______________
Disability Income	________	______________
Cash Gifts	________	______________
Trust Fund	________	______________
Other ________	________	______________
Other ________	________	______________
Other ________	________	______________
TOTAL	________	______________

Student Cash Flow Plan

Income

Monthly Income, after taxes________________

Item	Monthly Total	Actually Spent
Giving/Tithe	______	______
Saving	______	______
Housing/Rent	______	______
Renter's Insurance	______	______
*Food	______	______
Water	______	______
Gas	______	______
Electricity	______	______
Garbage	______	______
Phone	______	______
Mobile Phone	______	______
Internet Access	______	______
Car Payment	______	______
Car Insurance	______	______
*Gas & Oil	______	______
*Repairs & Tires	______	______
*Clothing	______	______
*Entertainment	______	______
Health Insurance	______	______
Miscellaneous	______	______
Total Necessities	______	______
Total Income		______
Minus Total Necessities		______
Equals		**$0.00 (Zero)**

*Use the Envelope System for these expenses.

Monthly Cash Flow Plan

Budgeted Item	Sub Total	TOTAL	Actually Spent	% of Take Home Pay
Charitable Gifts				
Saving		$300		10%
Emergency Fund				
Retirement Fund				
College Fund	$50			
Housing		$50		
First Mortgage				
Second Mortgage				
Real Estate Taxes	$725			
Homeowners Ins.				
Repairs or Maint. Fee				
Replace Furniture				
Other __________				
Utilities	$50	$775		
Electricity				
Water				
Gas	$100			
Phone	$50			
Trash	$50			
Cable	$50			
***Food**		$250		
*Grocery				
*Restaurants				
Transportation	$600			
Car Payment	$100	$700		
Car Payment				
*Gas and Oil				
*Repairs and Tires				
Car Insurance				
License and Taxes				
Car Replacement				
PAGE 1 TOTAL		**$2,075**		

Monthly Cash Flow Plan

Budgeted Item	Sub Total	TOTAL	Actually Spent	% of Take Home Pay
Charitable Gifts		______	______	______
Saving				
Emergency Fund	______		______	
Retirement Fund	______		______	
College Fund	______	______	______	______
Housing				
First Mortgage	______			
Second Mortgage	______		______	
Real Estate Taxes	______		______	
Homeowners Ins.	______		______	
Repairs or Maint. Fee	______		______	
Replace Furniture	______		______	
Other ______	______	______	______	______
Utilities				
Electricity	______		______	
Water	______		______	
Gas	______		______	
Phone	______		______	
Trash	______		______	
Cable	______	______	______	______
***Food**				
*Grocery	______		______	
*Restaurants	______	______	______	______
Transportation				
Car Payment	______		______	
Car Payment	______		______	
*Gas and Oil	______		______	
*Repairs and Tires	______		______	
Car Insurance	______		______	
License and Taxes	______		______	
Car Replacement	______	______	______	______
PAGE 1 TOTAL		______	______	

Monthly Cash Flow Plan

(continued)

Budgeted Item	Sub Total	TOTAL	Actually Spent	% of Take Home Pay
***Clothing**				
*Children	100			
*Adults				
*Cleaning/Laundry		100		
Medical/Health				
Disability Insurance	100			
Health Insurance				
Doctor Bills	50			
Dentist	20			
Optometrist				
Drugs		170		
Personal				
Life Insurance				
Child Care				
*Baby Sitter				
*Toiletries				
*Cosmetics				
*Hair Care				
Education/Adult				
School Tuition				
School Supplies				
Child Support				
Alimony				
Subscriptions				
Organization Dues	25			
Gifts (inc. Christmas)				
Miscellaneous	110			
***BLOW $$**	120	255		
PAGE 2 TOTAL		**525**		

Monthly Cash Flow Plan

(continued)

Budgeted Item	Sub Total	TOTAL	Actually Spent	% of Take Home Pay
***Clothing**				
*Children	______		______	
*Adults	______		______	
*Cleaning/Laundry	______	______	______	______
Medical/Health				
Disability Insurance	______		______	
Health Insurance	______		______	
Doctor Bills	______		______	
Dentist	______		______	
Optometrist	______		______	
Drugs	______	______	______	______
Personal				
Life Insurance	______		______	
Child Care	______		______	
*Baby Sitter	______		______	
*Toiletries	______		______	
*Cosmetics	______		______	
*Hair Care	______		______	
Education/Adult	______		______	
School Tuition	______		______	
School Supplies	______		______	
Child Support	______		______	
Alimony	______		______	
Subscriptions	______		______	
Organization Dues	______		______	
Gifts (inc. Christmas)	______		______	
Miscellaneous	______		______	
***BLOW $$**	______	______	______	______
PAGE 2 TOTAL		______		

Monthly Cash Flow Plan

(continued)

Budgeted Item	Sub Total	TOTAL	Actually Spent	% of Take Home Pay
Recreation				
*Entertainment	50			
Vacation	25	75		
Debts (Hopefully -0-)				
Visa 1	100			
Visa 2				
MasterCard 1	75			
MasterCard 2				
American Express	50			
Discover Card				
Gas Card 1				
Gas Card 2				
Dept. Store Card 1				
Dept. Store Card 2				
Finance Co. 1				
Finance Co. 2				
Credit Line				
Student Loan 1	100			
Student Loan 2				
Other ______				
Other ______				
Other ______				
Other ______				
Other ______		325		
PAGE 3 TOTAL		**400**		
PAGE 2 TOTAL		**525**		
PAGE 1 TOTAL		**2075**		
GRAND TOTAL		**3000**		
TOTAL HOUSEHOLD INCOME		**3000**		
		ZERO		

Monthly Cash Flow Plan

(continued)

Budgeted Item	**Sub Total**	**TOTAL**	**Actually Spent**	**% of Take Home Pay**
Recreation				
*Entertainment	______		______	
Vacation	______	______	______	______
Debts (Hopefully -0-)				
Visa 1	______		______	
Visa 2	______		______	
MasterCard 1	______		______	
MasterCard 2	______		______	
American Express	______		______	
Discover Card	______		______	
Gas Card 1	______		______	
Gas Card 2	______		______	
Dept. Store Card 1	______		______	
Dept. Store Card 2	______		______	
Finance Co. 1	______		______	
Finance Co. 2	______		______	
Credit Line	______		______	
Student Loan 1	______		______	
Student Loan 2	______		______	
Other ______	______		______	
Other ______	______		______	
Other ______	______		______	
Other ______	______		______	
Other ______	______	______	______	______
PAGE 3 TOTAL		______	______	
PAGE 2 TOTAL		______	______	
PAGE 1 TOTAL		______	______	
GRAND TOTAL		______	______	
TOTAL HOUSEHOLD INCOME		______		
		ZERO		

Recommended Budgeting Percentages

I have used a compilation of several sources and my own experience to derive the suggested percentage guidelines. However, these are only recommended percentages and will change dramatically if you have a very high or very low income. For instance, if you have a very low income, your necessities percentages will be high. If you have a high income your necessities will be a lower percentage of income and hopefully savings (not debt) will be higher than recommended.

ITEM	ACTUAL %	RECOMMENDED %
CHARITABLE GIFTS	___________	10-15%
SAVING	___________	5-10%
HOUSING	___________	25-35%
UTILITIES	___________	5-10%
FOOD	___________	5-15%
TRANSPORTATION	___________	10-15%
CLOTHING	___________	2-7%
MEDICAL/HEALTH	___________	5-10%
PERSONAL	___________	5-10%
RECREATION	___________	5-10%
DEBTS	___________	5-10%

Allocated Spending Plan

Getting Started

This sheet is where all your work thus far starts giving you some peace. You will implement your Cash Flow Plan information from theory into your life by using the Allocated Spending Plan. Note: If you have an irregular income, like self-employment or commissions, you should use the Irregular Income Form.

There are four columns to distribute as many as four different incomes within one month. Each column is one pay period.

If you are a one-income household and you get paid two times per month then you will only use two columns.

If you are married and both of you work and one is paid weekly and the other every two weeks, add the two paychecks together on the weeks you both get a paycheck, while just listing the one paycheck on the other two.

Date the pay period columns then enter the income for that period. As you allocate your paycheck to an item, put the remaining total balance to the right of the slash.

Using the examples, Income for period 3-1 is $1,000. We are allocating $100 to Charitable Giving leaving $900 to the right of the slash in that same column. Some bills will come out of each pay period and some only on selected pay periods. You already pay some bills or payments out of designated checks, only now you pay ALL things from designated checks.

The objective of this form is to focus all your monthly planning on one page: to allocate or "spend" your whole paycheck before you get paid. Allocate all of it before you get your check. No more management by crisis or impulse. Those who tend to be impulsive should just allocate more to the "Blow" category. At least you are now doing it on purpose and not by default.

The last blank that you make an entry in should have a "0" to the right of the slash, showing you have allocated your whole check.

An "*" beside an item means you should use the "envelope system."

Emergency Fund gets ALL the savings until 3-6 months of expenses have been saved.

SAMPLE ALLOCATED SPENDING PLAN FOUND ON NEXT PAGE

Allocated Spending Plan

PAY PERIOD:	8/1	8/8	8/15	8/22
ITEM				
Income	$650	$850	$1,500	0
Charitable	75/575	/	/	/
Saving				
Emergency Fund	50/525	/	/	/
Retirement Fund	/	/	/	/
College Fund	/	/	/	/
Housing				
First Mortgage	/	750/100	/	/
Second Mortgage	/	/	/	/
Real Estate Taxes	/	/	/	/
Homeowners Ins.	/	/	/	/
Repairs or Mn. Fees	/	/	/	/
Replace Furniture	50/475	/	/	/
Other _______	/	/	/	/
Utilities				
Electricity	100/375	/	/	/
Water	50/325	/	/	/
Gas	/	50/50	/	/
Phone	/	25/25	/	/
Trash	/	/	/	/
Cable	/	25/0	/	/
***Food**				
*Grocery	300/25	/	/	/
*Restaurants	25/0	/	/	/

Allocated Spending Plan

PAY PERIOD:	________	________	________	________
ITEM				
Income	____/____	____/____	____/____	____/____
Charitable	____/____	____/____	____/____	____/____
Saving				
Emergency Fund	____/____	____/____	____/____	____/____
Retirement Fund	____/____	____/____	____/____	____/____
College Fund	____/____	____/____	____/____	____/____
Housing				
First Mortgage	____/____	____/____	____/____	____/____
Second Mortgage	____/____	____/____	____/____	____/____
Real Estate Taxes	____/____	____/____	____/____	____/____
Homeowners Ins.	____/____	____/____	____/____	____/____
Repairs or Maint. Fees	____/____	____/____	____/____	____/____
Replace Furniture	____/____	____/____	____/____	____/____
Other ____________	____/____	____/____	____/____	____/____
Utilities				
Electricity	____/____	____/____	____/____	____/____
Water	____/____	____/____	____/____	____/____
Gas	____/____	____/____	____/____	____/____
Phone	____/____	____/____	____/____	____/____
Trash	____/____	____/____	____/____	____/____
Cable	____/____	____/____	____/____	____/____
***Food**				
*Grocery	____/____	____/____	____/____	____/____
*Restaurants	____/____	____/____	____/____	____/____

Allocated Spending Plan

Transportation				
Car Payment	____/____	____/____	____/____	____/____
Car Payment	____/____	____/____	____/____	____/____
*Gas and Oil	____/____	____/____	____/____	____/____
*Repairs and Tires	____/____	____/____	____/____	____/____
Car Insurance	____/____	____/____	____/____	____/____
License and Taxes	____/____	____/____	____/____	____/____
Car Replacement	____/____	____/____	____/____	____/____
***Clothing**				
*Children	____/____	____/____	____/____	____/____
*Adults	____/____	____/____	____/____	____/____
*Cleaning/Laundry	____/____	____/____	____/____	____/____
Medical/Health				
Disability Insurance	____/____	____/____	____/____	____/____
Health Insurance	____/____	____/____	____/____	____/____
Doctor	____/____	____/____	____/____	____/____
Dentist	____/____	____/____	____/____	____/____
Optometrist	____/____	____/____	____/____	____/____
Drugs	____/____	____/____	____/____	____/____
Personal				
Life Insurance	____/____	____/____	____/____	____/____
Child Care	____/____	____/____	____/____	____/____
*Baby Sitter	____/____	____/____	____/____	____/____
*Toiletries	____/____	____/____	____/____	____/____
*Cosmetics	____/____	____/____	____/____	____/____
*Hair Care	____/____	____/____	____/____	____/____
Education/Adult	____/____	____/____	____/____	____/____
School Tuition	____/____	____/____	____/____	____/____
School Supplies	____/____	____/____	____/____	____/____
Child Support	____/____	____/____	____/____	____/____

Allocated Spending Plan

Alimony	____/____	____/____	____/____	____/____
Subscriptions	____/____	____/____	____/____	____/____
Organization Dues	____/____	____/____	____/____	____/____
Gifts (inc.Christmas)	____/____	____/____	____/____	____/____
Miscellaneous	____/____	____/____	____/____	____/____
***BLOW $$**	____/____	____/____	____/____	____/____
Recreation				
*Entertainment	____/____	____/____	____/____	____/____
Vacation	____/____	____/____	____/____	____/____
Debts (Hopefully -0-)				
Visa 1	____/____	____/____	____/____	____/____
Visa 2	____/____	____/____	____/____	____/____
MasterCard 1	____/____	____/____	____/____	____/____
MasterCard 2	____/____	____/____	____/____	____/____
American Express	____/____	____/____	____/____	____/____
Discover Card	____/____	____/____	____/____	____/____
Gas Card 1	____/____	____/____	____/____	____/____
Gas Card 2	____/____	____/____	____/____	____/____
Dept. Store Card 1	____/____	____/____	____/____	____/____
Dept. Store Card 2	____/____	____/____	____/____	____/____
Finance Co. 1	____/____	____/____	____/____	____/____
Finance Co. 2	____/____	____/____	____/____	____/____
Credit Line	____/____	____/____	____/____	____/____
Student Loan 1	____/____	____/____	____/____	____/____
Student Loan 2	____/____	____/____	____/____	____/____
Other ________	____/____	____/____	____/____	____/____
Other ________	____/____	____/____	____/____	____/____
Other ________	____/____	____/____	____/____	____/____
Other ________	____/____	____/____	____/____	____/____
Other ________	____/____	____/____	____/____	____/____

Irregular Income Planning

Getting Started

Many of us have irregular incomes. If you are self-employed or work on commission or royalties, then planning your expenses is difficult especially since you can't always predict your income. Even though your income may fluctuate, you should still utilize all of the budgeting forms. Your Cash Flow Plan will tell you what you have to earn monthly to survive or prosper, and those real numbers are very good for goal setting.

Take the items from your Cash Flow Plan and prioritize them by importance. I repeat: by importance, not urgency. You should ask yourself, "If I only have enough money to pay one thing, what would that be?" Then ask, "If I only have enough money to pay one more thing, what will that be?" Move this way through the list. Now be prepared to stand your ground because things have a way of seeming important that are only urgent. Saving should be a high priority!

The third column, "Cumulative Amount," is the total of all amounts above that item. So, if you get a $2,000 check, you can see how far down your priority list you can go.

SAMPLE IRREGULAR INCOME PLANNING FORM FOUND ON NEXT PAGE

Irregular Income Planning

Item	Amount	Cumulative Amount
Penny's	$150	$150
Sears	$250	$400
Couch	$500	$900
Vacation - part	$200	$1,100
Christmas - part	$400	$1,500
Visa	$500	$2,000

Irregular Income Planning

Item	Amount	Cumulative Amount

Breakdown of Savings

After your emergency fund is fully funded, you can save for certain items like college, car, new stereo, or clothes, and your savings balance will grow. This sheet is designed to remind you that all of that money is committed to something, not just a Hawaiian vacation on impulse because you are now "rich." Keep up with your breakdown of savings monthly for one quarter at a time.

ITEM	BALANCE BY MONTH:	Sept.	Oct.	Nov.
Emergency Fund (1)	$1000			
Emergency Fund (2)	3-6 months			
Retirement Fund				
College Fund				
Real Estate Taxes				
Homeowners Insurance				
Repairs or Maint. Fee				
Replace Furniture		600	650	700
Car Insurance				
Car Replacement				
Disability Insurance				
Health Insurance				
Doctor				
Dentist		500	500	500
Optometrist				
Life Insurance				
School Tuition				
School Supplies				
Gifts (inc. Christmas)		600	700	800
Vacation		500	650	800
Other ________				
Other ________				
TOTAL		**2200**	**2500**	**2800**

Breakdown of Savings

After your emergency fund is fully funded, you can save for certain items like college, car, new stereo, or clothes, and your savings balance will grow. This sheet is designed to remind you that all of that money is committed to something, not just a Hawaiian vacation on impulse because you are now "rich." Keep up with your breakdown of savings monthly for one quarter at a time.

ITEM	**BALANCE BY MONTH:**	________	________	________
Emergency Fund (1)	$1000	________	________	________
Emergency Fund (2)	3-6 months	________	________	________
Retirement Fund		________	________	________
College Fund		________	________	________
Real Estate Taxes		________	________	________
Homeowners Insurance		________	________	________
Repairs or Mn. Fee		________	________	________
Replace Furniture		________	________	________
Car Insurance		________	________	________
Car Replacement		________	________	________
Disability Insurance		________	________	________
Health Insurance		________	________	________
Doctor		________	________	________
Dentist		________	________	________
Optometrist		________	________	________
Life Insurance		________	________	________
School Tuition		________	________	________
School Supplies		________	________	________
Gifts (inc. Christmas)		________	________	________
Vacation		________	________	________
Other ________		________	________	________
Other ________		________	________	________
TOTAL		________	________	________

Emergency Fund (1) is your first $1000 (or $500 if your income is less than $20,000). After completing your debt snowball, Emergency Fund (2) gets all of the savings until 3-6 months of expenses have been saved.

Consumer Equity Worksheet

ITEM / DESCRIBE	VALUE	-	DEBT	=	EQUITY
Real Estate ________	$90,000		$70,000		$20,000
Real Estate ________					
Car ______________					
Car ______________	$7,000		$10,000		- $3,000
Cash On Hand					
Checking Account					
Checking Account					
Savings Account	$1,000		0		$1,000
Savings Account					
Money Market Account					
Mutual Funds					
Retirement Plan	$7,000		0		$7,000
Cash Value (Insurance)					
Household Items					
Jewelry					
Antiques					
Boat					
Unsecured Debt (Neg)	0		$7,000		- $7,000
Credit Card Debt (Neg)					
Other ____________					
Other ____________					
Other ____________					
TOTAL	**$105,000**		**$87,000**		**$18,000**

SAMPLE

Consumer Equity Worksheet

ITEM / DESCRIBE	VALUE	-	DEBT	=	EQUITY
Real Estate ________	______		______		______
Real Estate ________	______		______		______
Car ____________	______		______		______
Car ____________	______		______		______
Cash On Hand	______		______		______
Checking Account	______		______		______
Checking Account	______		______		______
Savings Account	______		______		______
Savings Account	______		______		______
Money Market Account	______		______		______
Mutual Funds	______		______		______
Retirement Plan	______		______		______
Cash Value (Insurance)	______		______		______
Household Items	______		______		______
Jewelry	______		______		______
Antiques	______		______		______
Boat	______		______		______
Unsecured Debt (Neg)	______		______		______
Credit Card Debt (Neg)	______		______		______
Other ___________	______		______		______
Other ___________	______		______		______
Other ___________	______		______		______
TOTAL	**$**______		**$**______		**$**______

The Debt Snowball

Getting Started

List your debts in order from smallest to largest with the smallest payoff or balance first. Do not be concerned with interest rates or terms unless two debts have similar payoffs, then list the higher interest rate debt first. Paying the little debts off first shows you quick feedback, and you are more likely to stay with the plan.

Redo this sheet each time you pay off a debt so you can see how close you are getting to freedom. Keep the old sheets to wallpaper the bathroom in your new debt-free house. The "New Payment" is found by adding all the payments on the debts listed above that item to the payment you are working on, so you have compounding payments which will get you out of debt very quickly. "Payments Remaining" represents the number of payments remaining on that debt when you work down the snowball to that item. Cumulative Payments are the total payments needed, including the snowball, to payoff an item. In other words, this is your running total for "Payments Remaining."

Count down to freedom!

Date:_______________

Item	Total Payoff	Minimum Payment	New Payment	Payments Remaining	Cumulative Payments
Penny's	$150	$15	$0	0	Garage sale
Sears	$250	$10	$25	11	11
Visa	$500	$75	$100	PD	11
M.C.	$1,500	$90	$190	5	16
Car	$4,000	$210	$400	4	20
Stu. Loan	$4,000	$65	$465	6	26

TOTALLY Debt Free except the house!

Finish Emergency Fund; Fund Retirement/College; Then Payoff House

Count down to freedom!

Date:_______________

Item	Total Payoff	Minimum Payment	New Payment	Payments Remaining	Cumulative Payments

Pro-Rata Debts

Discover	$1,200	$150
Citibank Visa	300	45
MBNA Visa	200	25
Penny's	100	60
Sears	200	30
TOTAL	**$2,000**	**$310**

Income	$2,400
Necessity Expense	2,200
Disposable Income	**$ 200**

Can't Increase Income Anytime Soon

Pro-Rata Plan

SHEET 11

Item	Total Payoff	/	Total Debt	=	Percent	X	Disposable Income	=	New Payments
Discover	1,200	/	2000	=	. 60	X	200	=	120
Citibank	300	/	2000	=	. 15	X	200	=	30
MBNA	200	/	2000	=	. 10	X	200	=	20
Penny's	100	/	2000	=	. 5	X	200	=	10
Sears	200	/	2000	=	. 10	X	200	=	20

Pro-Rata Debts

If you cannot pay your creditors what they request, you should treat them all fairly and the same. You should pay even the ones who are not jerks and pay everyone as much as you can. Many creditors will accept a written plan and cut special deals with you as long as you are communicating, maybe even over-communicating, and sending them something.

Pro-Rata means "in proportion to; one's fare share": the percent of total debt each creditor represents. This will determine the amount needed to pay each creditor. Next, each month, send your payment, a copy of your budget and attach this sheet, even if the creditor says they will not accept it.

Item	**Total Payoff**	**/**	**Total Debt**	**=**	**Percent**	**X**	**Disposable Income**	**=**	**New Payments**
______	____	/	____	=	.____	X	____	=	____
______	____	/	____	=	.____	X	____	=	____
______	____	/	____	=	.____	X	____	=	____
______	____	/	____	=	.____	X	____	=	____
______	____	/	____	=	.____	X	____	=	____
______	____	/	____	=	.____	X	____	=	____
______	____	/	____	=	.____	X	____	=	____
______	____	/	____	=	.____	X	____	=	____
______	____	/	____	=	.____	X	____	=	____
______	____	/	____	=	.____	X	____	=	____
______	____	/	____	=	.____	X	____	=	____
______	____	/	____	=	.____	X	____	=	____
______	____	/	____	=	.____	X	____	=	____
______	____	/	____	=	.____	X	____	=	____
______	____	/	____	=	.____	X	____	=	____
______	____	/	____	=	.____	X	____	=	____

Sample Pro-Rata Letter

Date: Feb. 22, 2002

From: Joe and Suzie Public
123 Anystreet
Anytown, ST 11111

To: Mega Credit Card Company
999 Main Street
Big City, ST 00000

Re: Joe & Suzie Public # 1234-5678-9012-9999

Dear Collection Manager:

Recently, I lost my job. My wife is employed in a clerical position. We have met with a financial counselor to assess our present situation.

We acknowledge our indebtedness to you of $6000, and fully intend to pay you back in full. However, you are one of 6 creditors that we owe $42,968 to. We owe minimum payments of $782 each month. We are not able to meet these minimum payments at the present time, and we are not planning to go further in debt to meet these obligations.

We have put together a basic necessities cash flow plan based on our take-home pay of $2340 per month (see the enclosed copy of cash flow plan). Since we have 2 small children and no disposable income at this time to pay our creditors, we cannot make a payment to you at the present time but we do not intend to go bankrupt.

At this time, we ask for a moratorium on payments for the next 120 days. We will keep in close contact with you and, as soon as possible, we will begin making payments. If possible, we would like to request a reduction of interest during this time.

We are aware that this is an inconvenience to you, but we must meet the basic needs of our family first. We fully intend to pay our creditors all that we owe them. Please be patient with us. If you have any questions please contact us at 600-555-9876.

Thank you for your consideration of our present situation.

Sincerely,

Joe Public
Suzie Public

Credit Bureau Info

EXPERIAN (888) 397-3742
P.O. Box 2002
Allen, TX 75013
www.experian.com
Provides one free copy per year of your personal credit file; Additional copies are $7 each; Free copies are also available if you have been denied credit in the past 60 days and the creditor used their services.

EQUIFAX CREDIT BUREAU (800) 685-1111
P.O. Box 740241
Atlanta, GA 30374-0241
www.equifax.com
Copies of your personal credit file are available for a small fee ($0-$8) depending on your state of residence. Free copies are available if you have been denied credit in the past 60 days and the creditor used their services.

TRANSUNION CREDIT BUREAU (800) 888-4213
P.O. Box 2000
Chester, PA 19022
www.transunion.com
Copies of your personal credit file are available for $15 each depending on your state of residence. Free copies are available if you have been denied credit in the past 60 days and the creditor used their services.

Stop unauthorized direct mail marketing (including pre-approved credit card offers) and unwanted telemarketing calls!
How? First call 1-888-567-8688 and follow the instructions. To stop these offers for 2 years press 1; to permanently stop them, press 3.
OR: you can write a letter and request to be permanently removed from any pre-screening and direct marketing databases. Be sure to request that your phone number and address be permanently removed as well.

- For Direct Mailings:
  Direct Marketing Association
  P.O. Box 9008
  Farmingdale, NY 11735
- For Telemarketing:
  www.donotcall.gov
  (888) 382-1222

FEDERAL TRADE COMMISSION (202) 452-3245
Publishes a brief semi-annual list (March and September) on card pricing by the largest issuers for $5 per copy. Offers a number of free credit-related publications.

FEDERAL TRADE COMMISSION HEADQUARTERS (202) 326-2222
6th and Pennsylvania Avenue, N.W.
Washington, D.C. 20580
www.ftc.gov

Sample Removal Letter

Date ______________________________

(From)

____

____

____

VIA: Certified Mail, Return Receipt Requested
(To)
Direct Marketing Association
Mail Preference Service
P.O. Box 9008
Farmingdale, NY 11735-9008

RE: Unauthorized direct marketing and pre-approved credit card offers

This letter is your formal notice to remove my name from all direct marketing and pre-screening databases. I do not wish to receive any unsolicited offers, especially from credit card companies.

Not only do I request my name to be permanently removed, but also my phone number and address must likewise be permanently removed. My correct information is as follows:

(Complete name)
(Full address)

(Social Security Number)
(Phone number with area code)

Thank you for your immediate attention to this matter.

Sincerely,

(Signatures)

REQUEST FOR FILE DISCLOSURE
CREDIT BUREAU OF NASHVILLE
604 FOURTH AVE NORTH - P.O. BOX 190589 - NASHVILLE, TN 37219-0589

Reason for File Disclosure Request ______________________________

Referred by ______________________________ Was credit refused? yes no

I hereby request the Credit Bureau of Nashville to disclose to me the contents of my credit record. I understand that if I have been rejected for credit within the past sixty (60) days as the result of credit information contained in my credit record, there will be NO CHARGE for this disclosure, otherwise there will be an $8 charge for an individual disclosure or $10 for both myself and my spouse.

Name ______________________________ Phone No. ______________

Spouse's Name ______________________________

Present Address ______________________________

City ______________________________, State ____________ Zip Code ____________

Former Address ______________________________

City ______________________________, State ____________ Zip Code ____________

Date of Birth ______________ Social Security No. ______________

Employed By ______________________________

How Long? ______________ Position ______________

Former Employment ______________________________

Spouse's Date of Birth ______________ Social Security No. ______________

Spouse's Employment ______________________________

How Long? ______________ Position ______________

I hereby authorize the Credit Bureau of Nashville to review my credit record with me, to make any necessary investigation of my credit transactions and to furnish to its subscribers reports based thereon. In consideration of its undertaking to make such an investigation I authorize any business or organization to give full information and records about me.

I am the person named above and I understand that Federal Law provides that a person who obtains information from a consumer reporting agency under false pretenses shall be fined not more than $5,000 or imprisoned no more than 1 year or both.

Signed ______________________________ Date ______________

Telephone Number ______________ Ext ________ where I can be reached during normal working hours.

AUTHORIZATION FOR DISCLOSURE OF SPOUSE'S CREDIT RECORD

I, ______________________, certify that I am presently married to ______________________, and am acting in his/her behalf in reviewing the credit record information concerning them maintained by the Credit Bureau of Nashville.

Sample Cease & Desist Letter

Date ______________________________

(From)

____

____

____

VIA: Certified Mail, Return Receipt Requested

(To)

____

____

____

RE: ______________________________________

Dear ______________________,

This letter will serve as your legal notice under federal law that regulates the activities of collection agencies and their legal representatives.

You are hereby notified under provisions of Public Law 95-109, Section 805-C, THE FAIR DEBT COLLECTION PRACTICES ACT to hereby CEASE AND DESIST in any and all attempts to collect the above debt.

Your failure to do so WILL result in charges being filed against you with the state and federal regulatory agencies empowered with enforcement.

Please be further warned that if ANY derogatory information is placed on any credit reports after receipt of this notice, it too will result in action being taken against you.

PLEASE GIVE THIS MATTER THE ATTENTION IT DESERVES.

Sincerely,

____

(Signature)

Sample Credit Bureau Letter

Date ____________________________

(From)

____

____

____

(To)

_________________________________ Credit Bureau

____

____

RE: ____________________________________

In reviewing the attached credit bureau report issued by your agency, I have detected an error regarding the following account(s) in that it is reported inaccurately.

Company Name: ____

Account Number: ____

Under the provision set forth in the 1977 Federal Fair Credit Reporting Act, I hereby request your agency prove to me in writing the accuracy of the reporting of this account. Under the terms of The Act and succeeding court cases you have 30 days to prove such accuracy or remove the account entirely from my report, and I ask that you do so.

You will note that this letter was sent certified mail, and that I expect a response within the said thirty (30) day period. Should I not hear promptly from you, I will follow-up with whatever action necessary to cause my report to be corrected.

Please feel free to call me if you have any questions, my home phone number is ______________________________ and my office number is ______________________.

Sincerely,

____

(Signature)

Sample Creditor Letter

Date ______________________________

(From)

____

____

____

(To)

____

____

____

RE: ______________________________________

Dear __________________________,

I am writing to formally request that your firm (or any agency hired by your firm) no longer contact me at my place of employment: _______________________________.

My employer requests that calls such as yours must cease, and under the terms of the 1977 Federal Fair Debt Collection Practices Act, I formally demand all such calls to my place of employment cease. You will please take note that this letter was mailed certified mail, so I have proof that you are in receipt of this letter should legal action against you become necessary on this matter.

I am willing to pay the debt I owe you, and I will be in touch soon to work out arrangements.

Feel free to contact me at my home between ____________ a.m. and __________ p.m. at the following number _________________________ or by mail at my home address:

____

____.

Please give this matter the attention it deserves.

Sincerely,

____

(Signature)

Sample Credit History Report

How to Read Your Credit Report

SAMPLE

The Name and Address of the office you should contact if you have any questions or disagreement with your credit report

Please address all future correspondence to the address shown on the right.

CREDIT REPORTING OFFICE
BUSINESS ADDRESS
CITY, STATE 00000
PHONE NUMBER

I.D. Section
Your name, current address and other identifying information reported by your creditors.

JOHN DOE
123 HOME ADDRESS
CITY, STATE 00000

DATE 03/04/94
SOCIAL SECURITY NUMBER 123-45-6789
DATE OF BIRTH 04/19/57
SPOUSE JANE

CREDIT HISTORY

Credit History Section
List of both open and closed accounts.

- Company Name: The first item identifies the business that is reporting the information.
- Account Number: This is your account number with the company reporting.
- Whose Acct.: See explanation below.
- Date Opened: This is the month and year you opened the account with the credit grantor.
- Months Reviewed: Number of months account payment history has been reported.
- Date of Last Activity: This is the date of last activity on the account and may be the date of last payment or the date of last change.
- High Credit: The highest amount charged or the credit limit.
- Terms: Represents number of installments (M=Months) or monthly payments.
- Balance: The amount owed on the account at the time it was reported.
- Past Due: This figure indicates any amount past due at the time the information was reported.
- Status: (See explanation below.)
- Date Reported: Date of last account update.

Company Name	Account Number	Whose Acct.	Date Opened	Months Re-viewed	Date of Last Activity	High Credit	Terms	Items as of Date Reported: Balance	Past Due	Status	Date Reported
SEARS	11251514	J	05/86	66	12/93	3500		0		R1	02/94
AMOUNT IN H/C COLUMN IS CREDIT LIMIT											
CITIBANK	2953900000100473	I	11/86	48	11/93	9388	48M	0		I1	12/93
DINERS	355411251511	A	06/87	24	10/92	500		0		01	12/93
CLOSED ACCOUNT											
CHASE	54229778	I	05/85	48	01/94	5000	340	3000	680	R3	02/94

>>> PRIOR PAYING HISTORY - 30(03) 60(04) 90+(01) 08/92-R2, 02/92-R3, 10/91-R4 <<<

Number of times account was either 30/60/90 days past due. Date two most recent delinquencies occurred plus date of most severe delinquency.

Collection Agency Accounts
Accounts which your creditors turned over to a collection agency.

>>> COLLECTION REPORTED 06/90; ASSIGNED 09/89 TO PRO COLL (800) 555-1234
CLIENT-ABC HOSPITAL; AMOUNT-$978; STAT UNPAID 06/90; BALANCE-$978 06/90
DATE OF LAST ACTIVITY 09/89; INDIVIDUAL; ACCOUNT NUMBER 787652JC

>>>>>>>>>>>>>>>>>>> COLLECTION AGENCY TELEPHONE NUMBER(S) <<<<<<<<<<<<<<<<<<
PRO COLL (800) 555-1234

*******************PUBLIC RECORDS OR OTHER INFORMATION******************

Courthouse Records
Public Record items obtained from local, state and federal courts.

>>> LIEN FILED 03/92; FULTON CTY; CASE OR OTHER ID NUMBER-32114; AMOUNT-$26667;
CLASS-CITY/COUNTY; RELEASED 07/92; VERIFIED 09/93

>>> BANKRUPTCY FILED 12/89; NORTHERN DIST CT; CASE OR OTHER ID NUMBER-673HC12;
LIABILITIES-$15787; PERSONAL; INDIVIDUAL; DISCHARGED; ASSETS-$780

>>> JUDGMENT FILED 07/91; FULTON CTY; CASE OR OTHER ID NUMBER-898872; DEFENDANT-JOHN DOE AMOUNT-$8984; PLANTIFF-ABC REAL ESTATE; SATISFIED 03/92; VERIFIED 05/93

**********************ADDITIONAL INFORMATION***********************

Additional Information
Primarily consists of former addresses and employments reported by your creditors.

FORMER ADDRESS 456 JUPITER RD, ATLANTA, GA 30245

FORMER ADDRESS P.O. BOX 2138, SAVANNAH, GA 31406

LAST REPORTED EMPLOYMENT - ENGINEER, SPACE PATROL

************COMPANIES THAT REQUESTED YOUR CREDIT HISTORY************

Inquiry Section
List of businesses that have received your credit report in the last 24 months.

03/04/94	DISCLOSURE	02/12/94	MACYS
12/16/93	PRM VISA	08/01/93	AM CITIBANK
06/11/93	NATIONS BANK	04/29/93	GE CAPITAL
02/17/93	JC PENNEY	02/12/93	AR SEARS

THE FOLLOWING INQUIRIES ARE NOT REPORTED TO BUSINESSES:

PRM - This type of inquiry means that only your name and address were given to a credit grantor so they could offer you an application for credit. (PRM inquiries remain for six months.)

AM or **AR** - These inquiries indicate a periodic review of your credit history by one of your creditors. (AM and AR inquiries remain for six months.)

DISCLOSURE, ACIS or **UPDATE** - These inquiries indicate our activity in reponse to your contact with us for either a copy of your credit report or a request for research.

PRM, AM, AR, DISCLOSURE, ACIS and **UPDATE** inquiries do not show on credit reports that businesses receive, only on copies provided to you.

WHOSE ACCOUNT

Indicates who is responsible for the account and the type of participation you have with the account.

J = Joint
I = Individual
U = Undesignated
A = Authorized user
T = Terminated
M = Maker
C = Co-Maker/Co-Signer
B = On behalf of another person
S = Shared

STATUS

Type of Account

O = Open (entire balance due each month)
R = Revolving (payment amount variable)
I = Installment (fixed number of payments)

Timeliness of Payment

0 = Approved not used; too new to rate
1 = Paid as agreed
2 = 30+ days past due
3 = 60+ days past due
4 = 90+ days past due
5 = Pays or paid 120+ days past the due date; or collection account
7 = Making regular payments under wage earner plan or similar arrangement
8 = Repossession
9 = Charged off to bad debt

Form 102249R-6-95 USA

Video Fill-In-The-Blank Keys

Chapter 1:	Chapter 2:	Chapter 3:	Chapter 4:	Chapter 5:	Chapter 6:
Priority	Simple	Wealth	Active	Myth	Value System
First	Stupid	Favored	Cash Flow	Truth	Enough
Bills	Simple	Qualified plan	Checkbook	Marketed	Important
Emotion	Never	Individual	Living	Shift	Negotiating
Contentment	Never	Retirement	Carbon	Helping	Hunting
Amoral	Borrowed	Simplified	ATM	Destroyed	Self-esteem
Attitude	Spread	401(k)	Debit	Helping	Scorecard
Emergency	Around	403(b)	Bread	Repay	Fear
fund	Lowers	457	Water	Services	Terror
Purchases	Risk	Earned	Abuse	Greedy	Security
Wealth Building	Return	$3,000/$5,000	Worked	Rich	Money Fights
Now	Availability	$3,000/$5,000	Fear	Math	Value System
Unexpected	Less	Type	Leave	Payments	Unity
$1,000	Deposit	After	Out	How	Both
3	Low	Should	Complicate	Leasing	Both
6	7%	Choices	Do	Expensive	Gift
Money	High	Bracket	Live	Paid-for	Budget
Market	Ownership	Invested	Crisis	Used	Both
Protection	Value	Flexibility	Farther	New	Nerd
Earner	Dividends	Self	Money Fights	60%	Free
Touch	Debt	15%	Guilt	Tax	Poverty
First	You	Most	Shame	Debt	Impulse
Borrowing	Interest	Contract	Fear	Math	Stress
Sinking	Few	Great	Bounced	Extra	Myself
$4,000	Bond	Leave	Checks	15-year	Single
24%	Money	$700,000	Stress	Good	Control
$211	Fund	Separate	Over Spending	Foreclose	Accountability
24	Value	Borrow	Zero	Credit	Purchases
$5,064	Increased	40%	Envelope	Mortgage	Budget
$211	Long	40%		Rent	School's
18	Investment	20%		Debit	Your
0%	Cash	Amount		Credit	Commissions
$500	Savings	Roth		Debit	Powerful
Discipline	Fixed	Roth		Month	Work
Consistent	Variable	Plans		Month	Work
Time	Very	IRA's		Study	Example
40	Risk	Growth		Teenager	Debt
$100	Las Vegas	Transfer		Target	Container
12%		Listed		Saves	5-12
$1,176,477		Custodian		Con	Giving
Discipline		Custodian		Little	13-15
Explosion		529		Debt	Car
Interest		Freeze		Debt	College
		Low		Tool	Debt-Free
		Insurance		Lender	
		Savings		75%	
		Zero-Coupon		Save	
		Prepaid		Give	
				Borrowing	
				Money	
				Save	
				Prayer	
				Something	
				Job	
				Snowball	

Chapter 7:	**Chapter 8:**	**Chapter 9:**	**Chapter 10:**	**Chapter 11:**	**Chapter 12:**
Misrepresented	Money	Transfer	Retailer	3.2	Plan
Harm	Personal	Risk	Enormous	16-18	Your
Win	Financing	Homeowner's or Renter's	Curb	80%	Sales People
Everything	78%	Auto	More	85%	Telemarketers
Win	24%	Health	Multiple	Ourselves	Turnover
Afraid	TV	Disability	Not	Money	Emotion
Deal	Media	Life	Interview	Meaning	You
Truth	Positioning	Long-term care	Not	Purpose	8 AM
Cash	$300	Deductible	Forced	Accomplishment	9 PM
Emotional	Changes	Liability	Inflation	Ability	Work
Visual	Make	Collision	Free	Skills	Except
Immediacy	Purchase	Replacement	Unclean	Personality	Horrible
Power	Over-night	Umbrella	Lot	Traits	Bank
Shut	Motives	Deductible	MLS	Values	Wages
Good	Stuff	Stop	Neighborhood	Dreams	Paper
Good	Understand	MSA	Location	Passions	Pro-rata
Bad	Cost	Large	Location	Job	$10,000
Away	Counsel	Income	Location	Vocation	10
Patience		Trained	Water	Career	Several
Married		Occupational	View	Job	Slow-pay
Deals		Life	Elvis	Are Getting	7
Trade		Short	Street	Are Becoming	10
Services		65%	Floor	Personal	Inaccurate
Estate sales		Elimination	Home	Educational	50%
Individuals		Longer	Inspector	15%	1
Public auctions		Lower	Opinion	85%	2
Couponing		Nursing	Hate	Qualifications	Inaccuracies
Garage/Yard sales		60%	100%	Interviews	Certified
Flea markets		20%	25%	3-5	Entire
Repo lot		Death	15	15%	Complaints
Refunding		Death	10%	Introduction letter	
Foreclosures		Idea	High	Cover letter	
Pawn shops		Own	Transfer	Resume	
Classified ads		Term	Borrower	Phone follow-up	
Consignment sales		Cash value	35%	30-45	
		Permanent	Conventional	Objectives	
		Insured	Private	Part-time	
		Low	FHA	Monthly	
		Keeps	3%	Pay-off	
		Fees	More	Purchase	
		High	VA	Lump	
		Term	Better	Worth	
		Spouse	Owner		
		Options	Great		
		Burial			
		Credit			
		Credit			
		Card			
		Cancer			
		Death			
		Cash			
		Burial			
		Life			
		Duplicate			

glossary

401(k): A "qualified retirement plan" for corporations. (cash or deferred arrangement)

403(b): A "qualified retirement plan" for non-profit groups such as churches, hospitals, and schools. (cash or deferred arrangement)

457 Plan: This is a "deferred comp" retirement plan for state and local government employees.

529 Plan: A college savings plan that allows individuals to save on a tax-deferred basis in order to fund future college and graduate school expenses of a child or beneficiary. Generally sponsored by a state, they are professionally managed investments.

12b-1 Fee: An annual fee that some mutual funds charge to pay for marketing and distribution activities.

Accountability: Taking responsibility; an "accountability partner" assists people in making wise decisions about life and money.

Active: Money is very active…it is always moving and can be utilized in many ways.

Active Management: Portfolio management that seeks to exceed the returns of the financial markets. Active managers rely on research, market forecasts, and their own judgment and experience in making investment decisions.

Adjustable Rate Mortgage (ARM): Adjustable Rate Mortgage; these were brought on as a result of high interest rates in the early 1980's; banks wanted to transfer the risk of higher interest rates to the consumer, so with these loans you start out with a lower rate and it increases over time; you do not want to get an ARM.

Aggressive Growth Stock Mutual Fund: A mutual fund that seeks to provide maximum long-term capital growth from stock s of primarily smaller companies or narrow market segments. Dividend income is incidental. This is the most volatile fund; invested in smaller companies, it is also referred to as a Small-cap fund.

Allowance: To make exception for.

Ambition: One's goals and desires in life (i.e., career goals).

Amoral: Lacking morals; is neither good nor bad. Money is amoral…it can be use for good or bad.

Amortization Table: A table which shows how much of each payment will be applied toward principal and how much toward interest over the life of the loan. It also shows the gradual decrease of the loan balance until it reaches zero.

Annuity: A type of investment where the money is guaranteed by an insurance company; a savings plan through an insurance company.

Appraisal: An opinion of value.

Appreciation: In increase in value.

Annual Percentage Rate (APR): When financing, this is used to determine the percentage of interest one pays to the lender.

Asset:: Anything that is owned by an individual. With respect to saving and investing, assets are generally categorized as liquid (cash) and capital (investment) assets.

Asset Allocation: The process of deciding how your investment dollars will be apportioned among various classes of financial assets, such as stocks, bonds, and cash investments.

Asset Allocation Fund: A Type of "balanced" mutual fund whose investment advisor may change the fund's mix of stocks, bonds, or cash investments in an effort to find the best balance between risk and potential return.

Asset Classes: Major categories of financial assets, or securities. The three primary classes are common stocks, bonds, and cash investments.

Assumption Loan: This is when a potential home buyer pays the seller the equity in the home and then takes over the payments.

ATM Card: The Automated Teller Card allows you to make transactions at bank automated teller machines.

Auctions: A public sale in which property or items of merchandise are sold to the highest bidder; a great place to find deals. Be careful and do your research.

Auto Insurance: Insurance to protect a car owner in the event of an accident or damage to a vehicle. Make sure you have adequate liability with auto insurance!

Average Annual Return: The rate of return on investments averaged over a specific period of time. It is determined by adding together the rates of return for each year and dividing by the number of years in the calculation.

Baby Steps: The 7 steps to a healthy financial plan.

Back-End Load: A sales commission paid when the investor sells mutual funds shares. May also be called a redemption fee or a contingent deferred sales charge. Some funds gradually phase out backend loads over several years.

Balanced Fund: A Mutual fund that invests in more than one type of financial asset (stocks, bonds, and in some cases, cash investments).

Balloon Mortgage: Mortgage where for a set period of time, the interest is lower than normal, however, the entire loan amount becomes due at the end of the term of the loan.

Banks: Corporations chartered by state or federal government to offer numerous financial services such as checking and savings accounts, loans, and safe deposit boxes. The Federal Deposit Insurance Corporation (FDIC) insures accounts in federally chartered banks.

Bankrupt: To declare bankruptcy. See Bankruptcy.

Bankruptcy: A legal procedure for dealing with debt problems of individuals and businesses; specifically, a case filed under one of the chapters of title 11 of the United States Code (the Bankruptcy Code).

Bargains: These are deals obtained when negotiating and you pay a lesser price than asked for an item.

Beneficiary: The recipient of assets passed on from the death of a friend or relative.

Bill of Sale: A written document that transfers title to personal property.

Bond Mutual Fund: Mutual funds that buy and sell bonds.

Bond: A debt instrument where a company owes you money. The rate of return on these is low. A form of I.O.U. issued by corporations, government, or government agencies. The issuer makes regular interest payments on the bond and promises to pay back or redeem the face value of the bond, at a specified point in the future (called the maturity date). Bonds may be issued for terms of up to 30 or more years.

Break-even Analysis: A method used to evaluate whether or not it is fiscally responsible to make changes or additions in one's insurance deductible(s).

Budget: A cash flow plan; giving every dollar a name at the beginning of the month.

Buyer's Remorse: Regretting a purchase soon after making it.

Capital Gain: A positive difference between an asset's price when bought and its price when or if sold; the opposite of capital loss.

Capital Gains Distribution: Payment to mutual fund shareholders of any gains realized during the year on securities that have been sold at a profit. Capital gains are distributed on a "net" basis, after subtracting any capital losses for the year. When losses exceed gains for the year, the difference may | be carried forward and subtracted from future gains.

Capital Loss: A negative difference between an asset's price when bought and its price when or if sold; the opposite of capital gain.

Career: This is your line of work.

Cash Investments: Investments in interest-bearing bank deposits, money market instruments, and U.S. Treasury Bills or notes. These contain maturities ranging in income and capital gains of an investment.

Cash Value Insurance: Life insurance that is expensive in order to fund a savings plan within it.

Catastrophic: To have a major, negative financial event. For example: to lose your home due to a fire.

CD: Certificate of Deposit; usually at a bank; this is just a savings account with a little higher interest rate because you are agreeing to tie up your money for a little while—6 months, one year, etc.

Chapter 7 Bankruptcy: The chapter of the Bankruptcy Code providing for "liquidation," i.e., the sale of a debtor's nonexempt property and the distribution of the proceeds to creditors.

Chapter 11 Bankruptcy: A reorganization bankruptcy, usually involving a corporation or partnership. (A chapter 11 debtor usually proposes a plan of reorganization to keep its business alive and pay creditors over time)

Chapter 13 Bankruptcy: The chapter of the Bankruptcy Code providing for adjustment of debts of an individual with regular income. (Chapter 13 allows a debtor to keep property and pay debts over time, usually three to five years.)

Check Card: A type of card is issued by a bank and used to make purchases; the money comes directly out of your checking account.

Checking Account: Account set up to maintain your daily financial activities. Users can draft checks for payment, issue deposits into their accounts, and keep track of their debit card transactions through their checking account.

Claim: Paperwork filed with an insurance company in order to get them to cover a loss.

Co-insurance: In a health insurance policy, after you pay the deductible the insurance company pays a percentage and you pay a percentage; 80/20—insurance pays 80% and you pay 20%.

College Fund: Money set aside in investments that will grow for college expenses.

Collision: The portion of auto insurance that covers losses due to auto damage in an accident.

Commission: This is what you should pay children other than allowances; they do chores to earn money, as opposed to just handing them money without them working for it.

Commodities: A commodity is food, metal, or another fixed physical substance that investors buy or sell, usually via futures contracts.

Compensation: The total wage or salary and benefits that an employee receives.

Compound Interest: Interest paid on interest earned. Interest credited daily, monthly, quarterly, semi-annually, or annually on both principal and previously credited interest.

Comprehensive: Pays for damage to your car that is not a result of an accident.

Consignment Shop: Retail facility where people can sell their items and the owner of the facility retains a percentage of the sale.

Consumer: A person who buys and/ or uses a product.

Contact Letter: A letter informing a prospective employer that you are interested in working for their organization. Usually accompanied with a resume.

Contents Policy: An insurance policy that covers your possessions in a home or apartment.

Conventional Loan: These are loans obtained through the Federal National Mortgage Association (FNMA), which insures them against default; down payments range from 5-20% or more.

Co-pay: In regards to health insurance; paying a set amount per visit. Co-pay expenses will vary depending upon the policy.

Co-signing: Signing a note to guarantee someone else's loan; if they default on the loan, you have to pay.

Cottage Industries: In-home businesses.

Couponing: When you use coupons to save money on groceries.

Cover Letter: Similar to the Contact Letter, the Cover letter is used to inform the prospective employer of your interest and capabilities as they relate to the employment opportunity.

Coverage: Applies to the amount of protection you have through an insurance company in the event of a loss.

Credit: Money loaned

Credit Bureau: An agency which collects the credit history of consumers so that creditors can make decisions about granting of loans.

Credit Card: Tool used to finance a purchase.

Credit Disability: Insurance that pays for financed items or purchases if you become disabled and are unable to earn an income.

Credit Laws

Federal Fair Credit Reporting Act (FFCRA), 1971:
Federal law that covers the reporting of debt repayment information. It establishes when a credit reporting agency may provide a report to someone; states that obsolete information must be taken off (7 or 10 years); gives consumers the right to know what is in their credit report; requires that both a credit bureau and information provider (i.e., department store) have an obligation to correct incorrect information; gives consumers the right to dispute inaccurate information and add a 100-word statement to their report to explain accurate negative information; and gives consumers the right to know what credit bureau provided a report when they are turned down for credit.

Federal Fair Credit Billing Act (FFCBA), 1975:
Federal law that covers credit card billing problems. It applies to all open-end credit accounts (ie… credit cards, overdraft checking). States that consumers should send a written billing error notice to the creditor within 60 days (after receipt of first bill containing an error); creditor must acknowledge in 30 days; creditor must investigate; and creditor may not damage a consumer's credit rating while a dispute is pending.

Federal Fair Debt Collection Practices Act (FFDCPA), 1978:
Federal law that prohibits debt collectors from engaging in unfair, deceptive, or abusive practices when collecting debts. Collectors must send a written notice telling the amount owed and name of the creditor; collector may not contact consumer if he or she disputes in writing within 30 days (unless collector furnishes proof of the debt); collectors must identify themselves on the phone and can call only between 8 am and 9pm unless a consumer agrees to another time; and collectors cannot call consumers at work if they are told not to.

Equal Credit Opportunity Act, 1975:
Federal law that ensures that consumers are given an equal chance to receive credit. Prohibits discrimination on the basis of gender, race, marital status, religion, national origin, age, or receipt of public assistance. Lenders cannot ask about your plans for having children or refuse to consider consistently received alimony or child support payments as income. If you are denied credit, you have a legal right to know why.

Truth in Lending Act, 1969:
Federal law that mandates disclosure of information about the cost of credit. Both the finance charge (ie… all charges to borrow money, including interest) and the annual percentage rate or APR (i.e., the percentage cost of credit on a yearly basis) must be displayed prominently on forms and statements used by creditors. The law provides criminal penalties for willful violators, as well as civil remedies. It also protects you against unauthorized use of your credit card. If it is lost or stolen, the maximum amount you have to pay is $50.

Federal Fair Credit and Charge Card Disclosure Act (FFCCDA), 1989:
A part of the Truth in Lending Act that mandates a box on credit card applications that describes key features and costs (i.e., APR, grace period for purchases, minimum finance charge, balance calculation method, annual fees, transaction fees for cash advances, and penalty fees such as over the limit fees and late payment fees).

Credit Life: Insurance that pays for financed items or purchases in the event of your death.

Credit Report: Report showing your payment history.

Credit Union: Not-for-profit cooperatives of members with some type of common bond (i.e., employer) that provide a wide array of financial services, often at a lower cost than banks.

Curb Appeal: The appearance of a home from the street.

Currency: Money

Custodian: One who is responsible for an account listed in a minors name.

Day trading: Establishing and liquidating the same position or positions within one day's trading.

Debit Card: Linked with your checking account, this is a tools used to make purchases. Not to be confused with the credit card.

Debt Consolidation: Combining all debts into one lower monthly payment, thus extending the terms in most cases.

Debt Snowball: Listing your debts smallest to largest and paying minimums on all of them—then attacking the smallest with extra money that is available.

Debt-free Fund: A fund used to buy your children a house when they get married with a condition; they take what would have been a house payment and invest it.

Deductible: The amount you pay with an insurance company before they begin paying.

Deed: The legal document conveying title to a property.

Deflation: A broad, overall drop in the price of goods and services; the opposite of the more common inflation.

Delinquency: Short for "deed in lieu of foreclosure," this conveys title to the lender when the borrower is in default and wants to avoid foreclosure. The lender may or may not cease foreclosure activities if a borrower asks to provide a deed-in-lieu. Regardless of whether the lender accepts the deed-in-lieu, the avoidance and non-repayment of debt will most likely show on a credit history. What a deed-in-lieu may prevent is having the documents preparatory to a foreclosure being recorded and become a matter of public record.

Depreciation: A decline in the value of property; the opposite of appreciation.

Direct deposit service: A service that electronically transfers all or part of any recurring payment—including dividends, paychecks, pensions, and Social Security payments—directly to a shareholder's account.

Direct Transfer: Movement of tax-deferred retirement plan money from one qualified plan or custodian to another. No immediate tax liabilities or penalties are incurred, but there is an IRS reporting requirement.

Disability insurance: An insurance policy that insures a worker in the event of an occupational mishap resulting in disability. Insurance benefits compensate the injured worker for lost pay.

Discipline: The key to wealth building; you must be consistent over time.

Discount Points: In the mortgage industry, this term is usually used only in reference to government loans, meaning FHA and VA loans. Discount points refer to any "points" paid in addition to the one percent loan origination fee. A "point" is one percent of the loan amount.

Disposable Income: Amount of money left over after all necessities and expenses are paid.

Diversification: To spread around, thus lowering one's risk. Spreading your money among different classes of financial assets and among the securities of many issuers.

Dividend: These are stock profits that are paid out to shareholders.

Dividend Distribution: Payment of income to mutual fund shareholders from interest or dividends generated by the fund's investments.

Dollar Cost Averaging: Investing regular sums of money (i.e., $50) at regular time intervals (i.e., quarterly) regardless of whether security prices are moving up or down.

Down Payment: The part of the purchase price of a property that the buyer pays in cash and does not finance with a mortgage

Earned Income: Payment received for work, such as wages, salaries, commissions, and tips.

Educational Savings Account (ESA): This is an after-tax college fund that grows tax free; you may put up to $2,000 per year per child in this account depending on your annual income.

Elimination Period: The amount of time that lapses after your disability and before the insurance company begins to pay you.

Emergency Fund: Three to six months of expenses in readily available cash.

Employee Benefit: Something of value that an employee receives in addition to a wage or salary. Examples include health insurance, life insurance, discounted childcare, and subsidized meals at the company cafeteria.

Employer-Sponsored Retirement Savings Program: Tax-deferred savings plans offered by employers that provide a federal tax deduction, tax-deferral of contributions and earnings, and, in some cases, employer matching. They include 401(k) plans for corporate employees, 403(b) plans for employees of schools and non-profit organizations, and Section 457 plans for state and local government employees.

Employer Sponsored Savings Plan: A government approved program through which an employer can assist workers in building their personal retirement funds.

Empowerment: To gain strength emotionally and spiritually.

Entrepreneur: A person who starts a business.

Envelope System: A series of envelopes used to store cash for planned monthly expenses; a self-imposed discipline tool to assist people in managing their monthly finances. (i.e., putting a set amount of money into a "food" envelope to spend only on "food" for that month)

Equity: Your ownership portion of an item.

Estate Sale: Glorified yard sales with more items and higher prices. Usually, a great place for negotiating.

Exchange Privilege: The right to exchange shares in one fund for shares in another fund within the same fund family; typically at no charge or for a nominal fee.

Expense: The cost of a good or service.

Expense Ratio: The percentage of a fund's average net assets used to pay annual fund expenses. The expense ratio takes into account management fees, administrative fees and any 12b-1 marketing fees.

Federal Deposit Insurance Corporation (FDIC): A federal institution that insures bank deposits.

Federal Housing Administration (FHA): Federally sponsored agency chartered in 1934 whose stock is currently owned by savings institutions across the United States. The agency buys residential mortgages that meet certain requirements, sells these mortgages in packages, and insures the lenders against loss.

Federal Insurance Contributions Act (FICA): Government legislation that funds Social Security.

Federal Reserve System: The monetary authority of the US, established in 1913, and governed by the Federal Reserve Board located in Washington, D.C. The system includes 12 Federal Reserve Banks and is authorized to regulate monetary policy in the US as well as to supervise Federal Reserve member banks, bank holding companies, international operations of US banks, and US operations of foreign banks.

Fee Table: A Table, placed near the front of a mutual fund's prospectus, disclosing and illustrating the expenses and fees a shareholder will incur.

Financial Goals: Short-, immediate-, and long-term goals that require money and guide a person's future plans and savings decisions.

Financial Plan: A plan of action that allows a person to meet not only the immediate needs but also their long-term goals.

Financial Resources: Financial assets that can be accessed when necessary.

Financing: To buy an item with credit; paying over time.

Finite: Having a beginning and an end; money is finite—it has limits.

Fiscal: Having to do with money.

Fiscal Year (FY): Accounting period covering 12 consecutive months over which a company determines earnings and profits. The fiscal year serves as a period of reference for the company and does not necessarily correspond to the calendar year.

Fixed Annuity: A type of annuity that guarantees a certain rate of return—for example 6%; these are usually low and are not recommended for long-term wealth building.

Fixed Income Securities: Investments, such as bonds, which provide current income from a fixed schedule of interest payments. While the level of income offered by these securities is predetermined and usually stable, their market value may fluctuate.

Fixed Rate: An interest rate that does not change over time.

Floor Plan: The basic layout of a home.

Foreclosure: Process by which the holder of a mortgage seizes the property of a homeowner who has not made interest and/or principal payments on time as stipulated in the mortgage contract.

Fraud: A seller's intentional deception of a buyer, which is illegal.

Free Spirit: A spouse who thinks, "everything will work out fine."

Front-End Load: A sales commission or load which is paid when shares of a mutual fund are purchased.

Fund Family: A group of mutual funds sponsored by the same organization, often offering exchange privileges between funds and combined account statements for multiple funds.

Futures: A term used to designate all contracts covering the sale of financial instruments or physical commodities for future delivery on a commodity exchange.

Garnishee: A court ordered settlement that allows a lender to take monies owed directly from a borrower's paycheck.

Global Fund: A mutual fund that invests anywhere in the world, including the U.S.

Government Transfer Payments: Payments by governments, such as social security, veteran's benefits, and welfare, to people who do not supply current goods, services, or labor in exchange for these payments.

Grace Period: A time period during which a borrower can pay the full balance of credit due and not incur any finance charges.

Gratuity: An amount paid beyond what's required usually to express satisfaction with service quality; also known as a tip.

Gross Income: A person's total income prior to exclusions and deductions.

Gross National Product (GNP): Measures and economy's total income. It is equal to G.D.P. plus the income abroad accruing to domestic residents minus income generated in domestic market accruing to non-residents.

Growth and Income Mutual Fund: These are funds that buy stocks in larger more established companies; also called a Large-cap fund; they also contain medium sized companies or growth stocks.

Growth Stock Mutual Fund: These are funds that buy stocks in companies that are medium in size; they have grown, but are still expanding; also called Mid-cap funds.

Guaranteed Renewable: This means if you have a 20-year policy, the insurance has to provide coverage after 20 years regardless of health; it will only be more expensive because you are older.

Health Insurance: Covers you in the event of illness or injury.

Hoarding: Being greedy with an item such as money.

Home Equity Loan (HEL): Borrowing money using the equity from your home as collateral. A credit line offered by mortgage lenders allowing a homeowner a second mortgage that uses the equity present in the customer's account as collateral.

Home Inspector: An individual who inspects homes for defects prior the closing of a home sale to insure the buyer or lender's investment.

Home Warranty: An agreement that ensures the structural soundness of a home.

Homeowner's Insurance: Insurance that covers a loss due to damage, theft, or injury within your home.

House Poor: Having a house payment that is so high that it limits you in your ability to maintain it.

Impulse Purchase: To buy an item without thinking about it.

Income: Earnings from work or investment. (See compensation)

Income Fund: A mutual fund that invests in bonds and stocks with higher-than-average dividends.

Income Risk: The possibility that income from a mutual fund or other investment will decline; either as a fund's assets are reinvested or when a fixed income investment matures and is replaced with a lower-yielding investment.

Index: A statistical benchmark designed to reflect changes in financial markets or the economy. In investing, indexes are used to measure changes in segments of the stock and bond markets and as standards against which fund managers and investors can measure the performance of their investment portfolios.

Index Fund: A mutual fund that seeks to match the performance of a predetermined market benchmark, or index.

Individual Retirement Account (IRA): A tax-deferred account for individuals with earned income and their non-working spouses. Investment earnings with in an IRA are not taxed until money is withdrawn from an account. Contributions to an IRA may be deductible for income tax purposes.

Inflation: The rate at which the general level of prices for goods and services is rising. A broad, overall rise in the price of goods and services; the opposite of the less common deflation.

Inflation Hedge: Helps one to keep up with the rising cost of inflation. Real estate can be a great inflation hedge.

Integrity: Having to do with a person's honesty and moral attributes.

Interest: Money paid to savers and investors by financial institutions, governments, or corporations for the use of their money (example: 2% interest on money held in a savings account).

Interest rate: The monthly effective rate of interest on a loan.

Interest Rate Risk: The risk that a security of mutual fund will decline in price because of changes in market interest rates.

Internal Revenue Service (IRS): The federal agency responsible for the collection of federal taxes, including personal and corporate income taxes, Social Security taxes, and excise and gift taxes.

International Stock Mutual Fund: A mutual fund that contains companies that are International or over-seas.

Investing: The process of setting money aside to increase wealth overtime and accumulate funds for long-term financial goals such as retirement.

Investment: Where one would put their money for long-term growth. Suggested for a minimum of 5 years.

Investment Advisor/ Manager: The individual who manages a portfolio of investments. Also called a portfolio manager or a money manager.

Investment Horizon: The length of time you expect to keep a sum of money invested.

Investment Objective: A mutual fund's performance goal; such as long-term capital appreciation, high current income, or tax-exempt income.

Investors: People investing in securities, such as stock and bonds, to achieve long-term financial goals.

Job: A regular activity performed in exchange for payment, especially as one's trade, occupation, or profession.

Land Survey: A land survey is done to show where one's property lines are.

Large-cap Fund: These type of funds contain large, well established companies.

Lease: A long-term rental agreement, and a form of secured long-term debt.

Level Term: This means you pay the same amount for the entire term of the policy.

Liability: Covers you in the event someone brings a lawsuit against you due to injury on your property or as the result of an automobile accident.

Life Insurance: Insurance that covers or replaces income lost due to death.

Liquidity: The availability of money; as there is more liquidity, there is typically less return. The quality of an asset that permits it to be converted quickly into cash without loss of value.

Load fund: A mutual fund that sells shares with a sales charge-typically 4% to 8% of the net amount indicated. Some no-load funds also levy distribution fees permitted by Article 12b-1 of the Investment Company Act; these are typically 0. 25%. A true no-load fund has no sales charge.

Loan: Temporary borrowing of a sum of money. If you borrow $1 million you have taken out a loan for $1 million.

Loan To Value (LTV): What you owe vs. what you own. For example: a 70/30 LTV means that you owe 70% of the item's worth and you own 30%. Utilized with Private Mortgage Insurance (PMI).

Long Term Care Insurance: Covers the cost of nursing home or in-home care insurance. Recommended for people over the age of 60.

Long Term Coverage: Coverage for an extended period of time.

Loss: The negative difference between total revenue from a business or investment minus total expense.

Low- Load Fund: A mutual fund that charges a sales commission equal to 3% or less of the amount invested.

Lump Sum Savings: Saving money specifically for a purchase such as vacations or replacing cars, etc…

Management Fee: The fee paid by a mutual fund to its investment advisor.

Manager Risk: The possibility that a fund's investment advisor will do a poor job of selecting securities for the fund.

Market Risk: The possibility that an investment will fall in value due to a general decline in financial markets.

Maximum Pay: The amount an insurance company will pay before you are dropped from coverage. With health insurance keep at least a one million dollar maximum pay.

Medical Savings Account (MSA): A health insurance plan for self-employed people containing a large deductible. Money saved in this account grows tax deferred. It can be used for medical care with no penalties and not taxes and may be kept if unused.

Medicare: A federal government program of transfer payments for certain health care expenses for citizens 65 or older. The Social Security Administration manages the program.

Mid-cap Fund: A mutual fund containing a group of medium-sized companies that are growing.

Money: Currency and coin that are guaranteed as legal tender by the government.

Money Market Fund: Utilized for borrowing and lending money for three years or less. A mutual fund that seeks to maintain a stable share price and to earn current income by investing in interest-bearing instruments with short-term (usually 90 days or less) maturities.

Money order: A financial instrument backed by a deposit at a certain firm such as a bank that can be easily converted into cash.

Mortgage life insurance: A life insurance policy that pays off the remaining balance of the insured person's mortgage at death.

Mortgage: A loan secured by the collateral of some specified real estate property, which obliges the borrower to make a predetermined series of payments.

Multiple Listings Service (MLS): A computer program realtors use to find prospective homes for their clients.

Murphy's Law: Anything that can happen will happen.

Mutual Fund: Mutual funds are pools of money that are managed by an investment company. They offer investors a variety of goals, depending on the fund and its investment charter. Some funds, for example, seek to generate income on a regular basis. Others seek to preserve an investor's money. Still others seek to invest in companies that are growing at a rapid pace. Funds can impose a sales charge, or load, on investors when they buy or sell shares. Many funds these days are no load and impose no sales charge. Mutual funds are investment companies regulated by the Investment Company Act of 1940. Related: open-end fund, closed-end fund.

Myth: Information that has been passed on and is not true.

Needs: Those economic goods and services that are considered basic, such as food, clothing, and shelter.

Negotiating: To bargain for a lower price.

Nerd: One who is picky about budgeting and numbers.

Nest-Egg: What you have to live on financially after your income from employment stops.

Net Asset Value (NAV): The market value of a mutual fund's total assets, less its liabilities, divided by the number of outstanding shares.

No-load Mutual Fund: An open-end investment company whose shares are sold without a sales charge. There can be other distribution charges, however, such as Article 12B-1 fees. A true no-load fund has neither a sales charge nor a distribution fee.

Objective: A goal or plan.

Obsolete: No longer produced or in existence; not accepted as current.

Occupational Disability: Offers coverage in case you are unable to perform the job you were educated or trained to do.

Opportunity Cost: Determining whether a purchase is a need or a want and realizing that once the money has been spent, it is gone.

Out-of-Pocket: What YOU have to pay.

Owner Financing: Instead of paying a mortgage company, you pay the owner, who finances the purchase of the home; allows lots of flexibility.

Paradigm: Your belief system; the way you see or perceive things.

Part-time Job: A temporary job that allows you to supplement income.

Pawn Shop: Retail establishment selling items that have been traded as security for a cash loan; a great place to buy bargains.

Payroll Deduction: An amount subtracted from a paycheck as the government requires or the employee requests. Mandatory deductions include various taxes. Voluntary deductions include loan payments or deposits into saving accounts.

Permanent Disability: Disabilities that are ongoing.

Persistent: To be determined over time.

Points: See Discount Points

Policy: Describes the type of coverage within an insurance agreement.

Portfolio: A list of your investments.

Portfolio Transaction Costs: The costs associated with buying and selling securities, including commissions on trades, dealer mark-ups on bonds, bid-asking spreads, and any other miscellaneous expenses. These costs are not included in the expense ratio.

Preauthorized checking (PAC): Checking that is authorized by a payer in advance, and written either by the payee or by the payee's bank and then deposited in the payee's bank account.

Preauthorized electronic debits (PAD): Debits to a bank account in advance by the payer. The payer's bank sends payment to the payee's bank through the Automated Clearing House (ACH) system.

Pre-paid Tuition: Paying for college ahead of time by accumulating units of tuition; this is not recommended as your rate of return is only as much as the cost of tuition goes up as a result of inflation—on average about 6-7%.

Pre-tax Retirement Plan: A type of retirement plan where you put money in before taxes have been taken out but must pay taxes on the money at the time of withdrawal.
Principle:

Premiums: The amount you pay monthly, quarterly, semi-annually, or annually to purchase different types of insurance.

Principal: The original amount of money invested, excluding any interest or dividends. Also referred to as the face value of a loan, not including interest.

Priority: Level of importance. Saving must become a priority and you should always pay for your priorities or necessities first.

Private Mortgage Insurance (PMI): Policy protecting the holder against loss resulting from default on a mortgage loan.

Pro-active: To have a strong initiative; when one happens "to" things.

Procrastinating: To put off until later; waiting until the last minute.

Profit: The positive difference between total revenue from a business or investment minus total expense.

Prospectus: An official document that contains information required by the Securities & Exchange Commission to describe a mutual fund.

Purchasing Power: A measurement of the relative value of money in terms of the quality and quantity of goods and services it can buy. Inflation decreases purchasing power; deflation increases it.

Rate of Return: Also referred to as the "yield," this is the return on an investment expressed as a percentage of its cost.

Realtor: An intermediary who receives a commission for arranging and facilitating the sale of a property for a buyer or a seller. Also referred to as a Real Estate Broker or an Agent.

Reconcile: To work out; you should always reconcile your bank statement with your checkbook within 72 hours of receiving the statement.

Redemption Fee: A fee charged by some mutual funds for selling (redeeming) shares.

Refunding: Sending in proofs of purchase receive cash back or free gifts.

Reinvestment: Use of investment income or dividends to buy additional shares.

Rent: Periodic fee for the use of property.

Rental Real Estate: Buying real estate to rent out as an investment; make sure you have plenty of cash before doing this.

Renter's Insurance: Insurance that protects the possessions of one who rents a home or apartment.

Replacement Cost: Pays what it would cost to replace your home and the contents.

Repo Lot: A place where items that have been repossessed are offered for sale.

Resume: Personal and work history used for gaining employment.

Retailer: One who buys a product to resell.

Risk: Degree of uncertainty of return on an asset. In business, the likelihood of loss or reduced profit.

Risk Management: Procedures to minimize the adverse effect of a possible financial loss by: 1) identifying potential sources of loss; 2) measuring the financial consequences of a loss occurring; and 3) using controls to minimize actual losses or their financial consequences.

Risk Return Ratio: Relationship of substantial reward corresponding to the amount of risk taken.

Risk Tolerance: An investor's personal ability or willingness to endure declines in the prices of investments.

Rollover: Movement of a tax-deferred retirement plan's money from one qualified plan or custodian to another. No immediate tax liabilities or penalties are incurred, but there is an IRS reporting requirement.

Roth IRA: This is an after-tax investment where you have already paid tax on the money you are using but the investment grows tax-free.

Rule of 72: A quick way to calculate the length of time it will take to double a sum of money. Divide 72 by the expected interest rate to determine the number of years (ie… 72divided by 8% =9 years).

Rule of 78: Pre payment penalty (i.e., in 90 Days- Same as Cash deals, this is the portion of the loan agreement which states that the entire loan amount plus the interest earned over the first 90 days becomes due immediately).

Salary: Payment for work, usually calculated in periods of a week or longer. Salary is usually tied to the completion of specific duties over a minimum but not maximum number of hours. (see wage)

Savings: The process of setting aside money until a future date instead of spending it today. The goal of savings is to provide funds for emergencies, short-term goals, and investments.

Savings Account: Accounts at financial institutions that allow regular deposits and withdrawals. The minimum required deposit, fees charged, and interest rate paid varies among providers.

Savings Bond: A bond is a certificate representing a debt. A U.S. Savings Bond is a loan to the government. The Government agrees to repay the amount borrowed, with interest, to the bondholder. A government bond issued in face value denominations from $50 to $10,000, with local and state tax-free interest and semiannually adjusted interest rates.

Savings & Loan Associations (S & Ls): Financial institutions that provide loans and interest-bearing accounts. Accounts in federally chartered S & Ls are federally insured.

Sector Fund: A mutual fund that invests its shareholders' money in a relatively narrow market sector, e.g. technology, energy, the internet, or banking.

Self-Esteem: One's attitude about themselves.

Self-Insured: To insure one's self with personal assets.

Share: A piece of ownership in a company stock or mutual fund.

Short-term Disability: Disability for a minimal period of time.

Short-term Policy: Insurance policy that only covers a minimal amount of time.

Significant Purchase: Anything over $300.

Simple Interest: Interest credited daily, monthly, quarterly, semi-annually, or annually on principal only, not previously credited interest.

Simple IRA: A salary deduction plan for retirement benefits provided by some small companies with no more than 100 employees.

Simplified Employee Pension Plan (SEPP): A pension plan in which both the employee and the employer contribute to an individual retirement account. Also available to the self-employed.

Single Stock: Buying ownership in one company—the problem with single stocks is you are not diversified; there is a high degree of risk in single stocks.

Sinking Fund: Saving money to allow interest to work for you rather than against you.

Small-Cap Fund: A mutual fund that invests in companies whose market value is less than about $1 billion. Mutual funds that buy and sell smaller more volatile companies; also known as an Aggressive Growth Stock Mutual Fund.

Social Security: A federal government program of transfer payments for retirement, disability, or the loss of income from a parent or guardian. Funds come from a tax on income, a payroll deduction labeled "FICA."

Speculative: Purchasing risky investments that present the possibility of large profits, but also pose a higher-than-average possibility of loss.

Stock Markets:

National Association of Securities Dealers Automated Quotation System (NASDAQ)
The electronic stock exchange run by the National Association of Securities Dealers for over-the-counter trading. Established in 1971, it is America's fastest growing stock market and a leader in trading foreign securities and technology shares as well. The NASDAQ uses market makers who trade for their own account and profit on the spread between bid and ask prices. Although once the province of smaller companies, NASDAQ today is where many leading companies are traded, including Microsoft, Intel, MCI, Amgen, Cisco Systems, Nordstrom, Oracle, McCormick, SAFECO Insurance, Sun Microsystems, T. Rowe Price, Tyson Foods and Northwest Airlines.

New York Stock Exchange (NYSE)
The New York Stock Exchange traces its origins back more than 200 years, to the signing of the Buttonwood Agreement by 24 New York City stockbrokers and merchants in 1792. The NYSE utilizes a trading floor for traditional exchanges where buyers and sellers meet directly – that is, brokers representing investors on each side of the transaction come together on price. Centuries of growth and innovation later, the NYSE remains the world's foremost securities marketplace.

Stocks: Securities that represent part ownership or equity in a corporation. Each share of stock is a claim on its proportionate stake in the corporation's assets and profits; some of which may be paid out as dividends.

Stop-Loss: Your total out-of-pocket expense for health insurance; once reached, insurance will pay 100%.

Stuffitis: The wrong priority of 'stuff' in your life; to be overly materialistic.

Take-home Pay: The amount of money one has available after taxes have been taken out of their pay. Total wage, salary, commissions, and/ or bonuses minus payroll deductions.

Tax: A government fee on business and individual income, activities, products, or services.

Tax Credit: An amount that a taxpayer who meets certain criteria can subtract from tax owed. Examples include a credit for earned income below a certain limit and for a qualified post-secondary school expenses. (see tax deduction, tax exemption)

Tax Deduction: An expense that a taxpayer is allowed to deduct from taxable income. Examples include deductions for home mortgage interest and for charitable fights. (see tax credit, tax exemption)

Tax-Deductible: The effect of creating a tax deduction, such as charitable contributions and mortgage interest.

Tax-Deferred Income: Dividends, interest, and unrealized capital gains on investments in an account such as a qualified retirement plan, where income is not subject to taxation until a withdrawal is made. Investments where taxes due on the amount invested and/or its earnings are postponed until funds are withdrawn, usually at retirement.

Tax-Exempt (tax-free): Investments whose earnings are free from tax liability.

Tax-Exemptions: An amount that a taxpayer who meets certain criteria can subtract from a taxable income. Examples include exemptions for each dependent or for life insurance proceeds. (See tax credit, tax deduction.)

Tax Favored Dollars: Money that is working for you, either tax-deferred or tax-free, within a retirement plan.

Taxable Income: Income subject to tax; total income adjusted for deductions, exemptions, and credits.

Term Insurance: This is life insurance for a specified period of time; this is less expensive than cash value and is what is recommended for life insurance coverage.

Time Poverty: Having very little time to manage daily activities.

Time Value of Money: Comparison of a lump sum of money, or a series of equal payments, between two different time periods (i.e., present and future), assuming a specified interest rate and time period. (Reference: The Time Value of Money by Clayton and Spivey)

Tip: An amount paid beyond what's required, usually to express satisfaction with service quality; also known as gratuity.

Title Insurance: Insurance policy that protects a policyholder from future challenges to the title claim a property that may result in loss of the property.

Total Return: The change in percentage over a particular period in the value of an investment; including any income from the investment and any change in its market value.

Track Record: The past history of something; with investments, check at least the 5 or 10 year track record.

Transfer Payments: (See government transfer payments)

Turnover Rate: A measure of a mutual fund's trading activity. Turnover is calculated by taking the lesser of the fund's total purchases or total sales of securities (not counting securities with maturities under one year) and dividing by the average monthly assets. (e.g. a turnover rate of 50% means that, during a year, a fund has sold and replaced securities with a value equal to 50% of the fund's average net assets).

Uniform Gifts to Minors Act (UGMA): Legislation that provides a tax-effective manner of transferring property to minors without the complications of trusts or guardianship restrictions.

Unrealized Capital Gain/ Loss: an increase (or decrease) in the value of a stock or other security (mutual fund) that is not "realized" because the security has not yet been sold for a gain or loss.

Umbrella: Provides extra liability; once your assets are above $200,000, you should consider this.

Underwriter: A firm, usually an investment bank, that buys an issue of securities from a company and resells it to investors. In general, A party that guarantees the proceeds to the firm from a security sale, thereby in effect taking ownership of the securities.

Unearned Income: Money received for which no exchange was made, such as a gift.

Universal Life: Similar to cash value life insurance, but project better returns; this is not recommended as the type of life insurance to purchase.

Uniform Transfers to Minors Act (UTMA): A law similar to the Uniform Gifts to Minors Act that extends the definition of gifts to include real estate, paintings, royalties, and patents.

VA Loan: Designed to benefit veterans; allow a true zero-down purchase.

Value Fund: A mutual fund that emphasizes stocks of companies whose growth prospects are generally regarded as sub-par by the market. Reflecting these market expectations, the prices of value stocks typically are below average in comparison with such factors as revenue, earnings, book value and dividends.

Value System: One's priorities and things deemed important.

Variable Annuity: An annuity that has a varying rate of return based on the mutual funds you have invested in; this is better than the fixed annuity.

Variable Life: Similar to cash value life insurance, but will buy into mutual funds to project better returns; this is not recommended as the type of life insurance to buy.

Viatical: Of or relating to a contractual arrangement in which a business buys life insurance policies from terminally ill patients for a percentage of the face value.

Vocation: What you do for a living that is your "calling".

Volatility: The fluctuations in market value of a mutual fund or other security. The greater a fund's volatility, the wider the fluctuations between its high and low prices.

Wage: Payment for work, usually as calculated in periods of an hour rather than longer. (See salary)

Walkaway Power: In negotiating, this is the ability to walk away from a purchase.

Wants: Desires for economic goods or services, not necessarily accompanied by the power to satisfy them.

Wealth: Accumulated assets such as money and/ or possessions, often as a result of saving and investing.

Whole Life Insurance: Another name for cash value insurance; this is more expensive than term in order to fund a savings plan within the insurance; not recommended as the type of life insurance you need.

Win-Win Deal: Setting up a negotiation where both parties benefit.

Work Ethic: How motivated you are in your work.

Yield: The annualized rate at which an investment earns income, expressed as a percentage of the investment's current price.

Zero-coupon bond: A bond in which no periodic coupon is paid over the life of the contract. Instead, both the principal and the interest are paid at the maturity date.

Zero-based Budget: A cash flow plan where you spend every dollar on paper before the month begins.

Peace Puppies

1. **Avoid "Stuffitis"**--The Worship of "Stuff"
2. **Plant Seeds**--Give Money Away to Worthy Causes
3. Develop Your Own **"Power Over Purchase"**
4. **Find Where You Are Naturally Gifted**--Enjoy Your Work and Work Hard
5. **Live Substantially Below Your Income**
6. **Sacrifice Now** So You Can Have Peace Later
7. **You Can Always Spend More Than You Can Make**
8. **The Borrower Is the Servant to the Lender**; So Beware!
9. **Check Your Credit Report** at Least Once Every Two Years
10. **Handle Credit Report Corrections Yourself**
11. Realize That the Best Way for Delinquent Debt to Be Paid Is for You, Not Collectors, to **Control Your Financial Destiny**
12. **You Must Save Money** (the Power of Compound Interest)
13. Use the **"Keep It Simple, Stupid"** Rule of Investing
14. **Only People Who Like Dog Food Don't Save for Retirement**
15. **Always Save with Pretax Dollars**--It Is the Best Deal the Government Gives You
16. **Learn Basic Negotiating Skills** for Great Buys
17. **Learn Where to Find Great Buys** (the Treasure Hunt)
18. **You Must Have Patience** to Get Great Buys
19. **Singles Get Self-Accountability from the Written Plan**

20. **Singles Should Look for a Money Mentor for Advice and Accountability**

21. **Singles Beware of the Impulse Monster; He Will Eat You Alive**

22. **Men and Women View Money Differently, So Be Sensitive to Differences**

23. **Opposites Attract in Marriage, So Work Together for Maximum Wisdom**

24. **When You Agree on Spending, You Will Experience Fabulous Unity in Your Marriage**

25. **Teach Children to Work, Spend Wisely, Save, and Give**

26. **The Most Powerful Legacy You Can Leave Is Wise, Competent Children**

27. **Giving Loved Ones All the Money They Request May Not Be Best for Them**

28. **Making Decisions Based on Fear of Reprisal Can Be a Sign of Codependence**

29. **Be Strong Enough to Help Others and Strong Enough Not To**

30. **Listen to Your Spouse's Counsel** (Women's Intuition)

31. There Are Few "Old" Fools--**Seek Experienced Counsel**

32. **You Must Keep Your Checkbook on a Timely Basis**

33. Lay Out the Written Details of a **Cash Management Plan**

34. **Commit** to Your Plan for Ninety Days

35. **Take Time To Prioritize** Your Life Daily

36. **Keep Your Spiritual Life Healthy**

37. **Take Baby Steps**--Prioritize Your Plan and Move Slowly

Searching For Savings

C	G	A	L	W	D	C	W	S	V	V	F	Y	O	G
A	B	G	A	A	K	N	Z	E	I	O	C	U	H	N
P	K	Q	C	W	A	K	U	M	A	N	Z	O	U	I
M	Z	I	I	W	A	D	E	O	E	L	A	J	M	K
U	A	R	T	R	E	L	U	G	P	R	T	O	H	N
R	V	V	A	W	O	X	R	O	D	M	N	H	F	I
P	P	F	M	G	L	E	R	I	R	E	O	R	W	S
H	R	Z	E	J	M	V	N	L	Y	R	Y	C	N	P
Y	I	A	H	E	H	G	A	M	O	R	A	L	U	T
E	O	K	T	P	U	R	C	H	A	S	E	S	E	C
M	R	B	A	T	S	E	R	E	T	N	I	K	I	X
O	I	O	M	D	N	U	F	X	E	F	R	O	L	Y
B	T	N	S	N	L	M	W	G	D	A	C	E	N	G
N	Y	V	K	H	F	L	T	A	M	C	V	V	O	P
F	D	I	G	S	V	F	I	W	I	R	Z	V	U	P

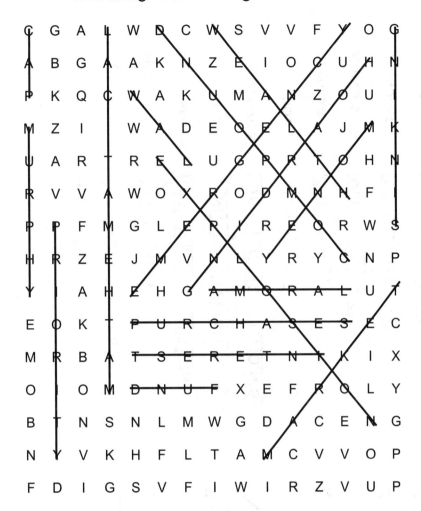

Risk And Reward

Similar to the TV game show, Wheel of Fortune, fill in the blanks to reveal a message. Letters appear in random order, there is no "code."

A	B	C	D	E	F	G	H	I	J	K	L	M	N	O	P	Q	R	S	T	U	V	W	X	Y	Z
22	26	18	7	16		3	2	11		4	8	6	9	25	12		21	17	24	14		5		13	

B E H O L D   T H E   T U R T L E   W H O
26 16 2 25 8 7   24 2 16   24 14 21 24 8 16   5 2 25

O N L Y   M A K E S   P R O G R E S S   W H E N
25 9 8 13   6 22 4 16 17   12 21 25 3 21 16 17 17   5 2 16 9

H E   S T I C K S   H I S   N E C K   O U T
2 16   17 24 11 18 4 17   2 11 17   9 16 18 4   25 14 24

I ll Pass On The Dog Food Thanks!

Unscramble each of the clue words. Then, reveal the hidden message, by copying the letters in the numbered cells to the empty spaces at the bottom of the page.

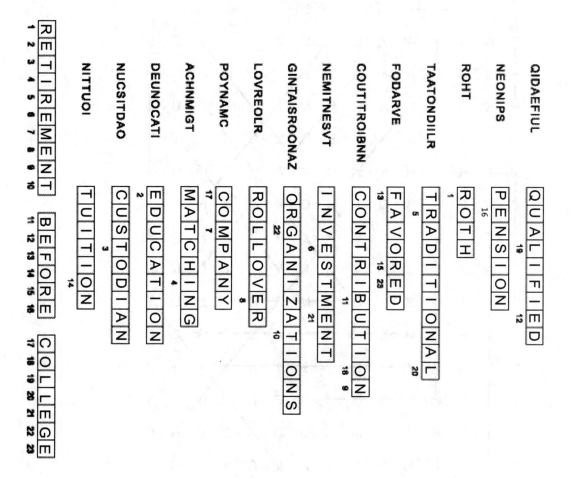

Clue	Answer	Numbered cells
QIDAEFIUL	QUALIFIED	L = 19, E = 12
NEONIPS	PENSION	E = 16
ROHT	ROTH	R = 1
TAATONDIILR	TRADITIONAL	R = 5, L = 20
FODARVE	FAVORED	F = 13, R = 15, E = 23
COUTITROIBNN	CONTRIBUTION	B = 11, O = 18, N = 9
NEMITNESVT	INVESTMENT	V = 6, E = 21
GINTAISROONAZ	ORGANIZATIONS	G = 22, T = 10
LOVREOLR	ROLLOVER	E = 8
POYNAMC	COMPANY	C = 17, M = 7
ACHNMIGT	MATCHING	I = 4
DEUNOCATI	EDUCATION	E = 2
NUCSITDAO	CUSTODIAN	T = 3
NITTUOI	TUITION	O = 14

1	2	3	4	5	6	7	8	9	10		11	12	13	14	15	16		17	18	19	20	21	22	23
R	E	T	I	R	E	M	E	N	T		B	E	F	O	R	E		C	O	L	L	E	G	E

Go With The Flow

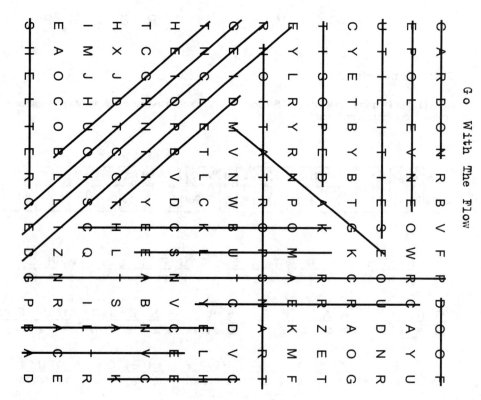

C	A	R	B	O	N	R	B	V	F	P	D	O	O	F
E	P	O	L	E	V	N	E	O	W	R	C	A	Y	U
U	T	I	L	I	T	I	E	S	E	O	U	D	N	R
C	Y	E	T	B	Y	B	T	G	K	C	R	A	O	G
T	I	S	O	P	E	D	A	K	I	R	R	Z	E	T
E	Y	L	R	Y	R	N	P	O	M	A	E	K	M	F
R	N	O	I	T	A	T	R	O	P	S	N	A	R	T
G	E	I	D	M	V	N	W	B	U	T	C	D	V	C
T	N	C	L	E	T	L	C	K	L	I	Y	E	L	H
H	E	I	O	P	B	V	D	C	S	N	V	C	E	E
T	C	G	H	N	I	I	Y	E	E	A	B	N	V	C
H	X	J	D	T	C	C	T	H	L	T	S	A	T	K
I	M	J	H	U	O	I	S	C	Q	I	I	L	T	R
E	A	O	C	O	B	L	L	I	Z	N	R	A	C	E
S	H	E	L	T	E	R	C	E	D	G	P	B	A	D

Shark Alert!

F	T	C	D	D	J	D	D	F	N	O	B	O	N	M
Q	I	R	O	N	T	A	E	C	O	E	B	O	E	O
L	A	N	J	S	B	K	N	B		H	I	W	Q	R
C	L	U	A	O	I	O	S	P	T	T	E	U	U	T
E	K	A	R	N	O	G	A	L	A	C	C	R		G
O	S	R	B	L	C	Y	N	I	D	H	N	N	T	A
P	O	A	L	W	M	E	C	J		T	A	K	Y	G
W	N	A	E	E	O	E	S	G	L	Y	V	U	D	E
R	B	V	N	L	R	N	D	C	O	M	D	X	G	X
A	Q	T	R	P	V	U	S	F	S	U	A	I	B	H
B	S	F	E	R	E	S	P	O	N	S	I	B	L	E
N	S	D	C	R	E	D	I	T	O	H	T	U	R	T
E	M	I	T	R	E	V	O	P	C	O	C	A	S	H
D	L	Z	S	R	X	R	Y	Q	K	E	U	I	Y	Y
E	B	I	J	L	W	G	U	U	G	Z	C	V	K	Y

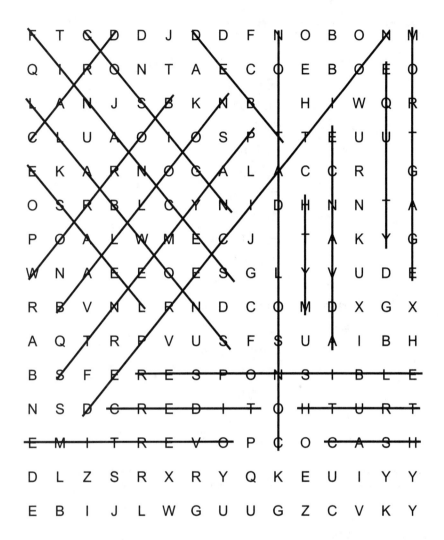

Teach The Children

Unscramble the tiles to reveal a message.

.	EN	NOT	LL	N T	WAY	HE	IS
D I	SH	AND	OUL	HE	PAR	UP	HIL
IN	O,	HE	IT	D G	T F	DE	TRA
A C	WH	HE	OLD	WI	ROM		

TRA	IN	UP	A C	HILD		IN	THE
WAY	HE	SH	OUL	D G	O	AND	WH
EN	HE	IS	OLD	HE	WI	LL	NOT
DE	PAR	T F	ROM	IT	.		

Bargain Bonanza!

Unscramble each of the clue words. Then, reveal the hidden message, by copying the letters in the numbered cells to the empty spaces at the bottom of the page.

Clue	Answer	Numbered cells
MEENERRDIESPST	MISREPRESENTED	R 11, R 18
GUTHINN	HUNTING	H 23, T 5
GANNOGIIETT	NEGOTIATING	O 2, T 27
RIELAT	RETAIL	R 26, A 8
SAHC	CASH	A 25, S 14
LIUVAS	VISUAL	I 28, U 10
POERW	POWER	W 15, R 22
CUEHQNETI	TECHNIQUE	H 16
LEMOANIOT	EMOTIONAL	E 17
MIACIMDEY	IMMEDIACY	Y 1
TOUCINA	AUCTION	U 21, I 13
NUOPCGION	COUPONING	O 20
NECPEITA	PATIENCE	E 24, E 7
VICESSER	SERVICES	S 29, R 4
TESTAE	ESTATE	E 12
LAVDUIDIINS	INDIVIDUALS	U 3
CAFSSLIDSEI	CLASSIFIEDS	S 9, E 19
GEURNNFDI	REFUNDING	R 6

YOUR TREASURE IS WHERE YOUR HEART IS

Y	O	U	R	T	R	E	A	S	U	R	E	I	S	W	H	E	R	E	Y	O	U	R	H	E	A	R	T	I	S
1	2	3	4	5	6	7	8	9	10	11	12	13	14	15	16	17	18	19	1	20	21	22	23	24	25	26	27	28	29

Watch Your Step

Rearrange the letters into their appropriate column to reveal a message. Letters can only be used with in the column directly above them.

*Spaces containing punctuation marks do not require a letter.

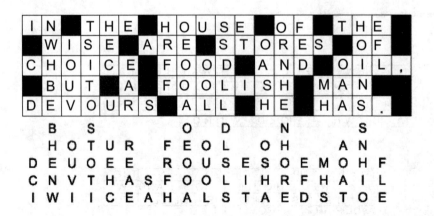

I	N	■	T	H	E	■	H	O	U	S	E	■	O	F	■	T	H	E	■
■	W	I	S	E	■	A	R	E	■	S	T	O	R	E	S	■	O	F	■
C	H	O	I	C	E	■	F	O	O	D	■	A	N	D	■	O	I	L	,
■	B	U	T	■	A	■	F	O	O	L	I	S	H	■	M	A	N	■	■
D	E	V	O	U	R	S	■	A	L	L	■	H	E	■	H	A	S	.	■
	B		S						O	D			N				S		
	H	O	T	U	R		F	E	O	L		O	H			A	N		
D	E	U	O	E	E		R	O	U	S	E	S	O	E	M	O	H	F	
C	N	V	T	H	A	S	F	O	O	L	I	H	R	F	H	A	I	L	
I	W	I	I	C	E	A	H	A	L	S	T	A	E	D	S	T	O	E	

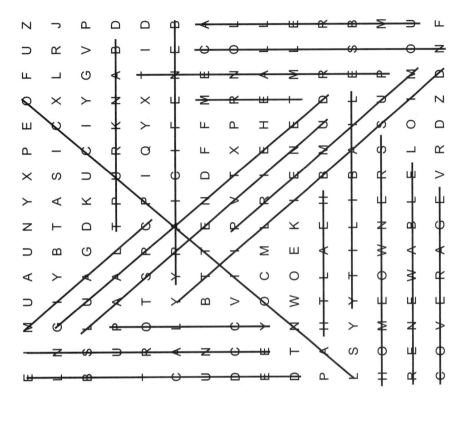

Mortgage Mania

Unscramble each of the clue words. Then, reveal the hidden message, by copying the letters in the numbered cells to the empty spaces at the bottom of the page.

Clue	Answer	Numbered cells
SARPAPLAI	APPRAISAL	11
ETRILERA	RETAILER	5
ARLOETR	REALTOR	12
CIAPEAPERT	APPRECIATE	15
NEVNACTOOLIN	CONVENTIONAL	2
CETSIPNOR	INSPECTOR	7, 17
LAFNINTOI	INFLATION	14
WRTAANYR	WARRANTY	8
NERWO	OWNER	9
SYREVU	SURVEY	16, 13
RAGTOGEM	MORTGAGE	10
CNNAFNIIG	FINANCIAL	1
BALDASJEUT	ADJUSTABLE	4
TAER	RATE	6
FIDXE	FIXED	3

FIFTEEN YEAR OR LESS
1 2 3 4 5 6 7 8 9 10 11 12 13 14 15 16 17

Insuring Your Future

E	I	M	U	A	U	N	Y	X	P	E	O	F	U	Z
L	N	G	I	Y	B	T	A	S	I	C	X	L	R	J
B	S	L	U	A	G	D	K	U	C	I	Y	G	V	P
I	U	P	A	A	L	T	P	U	R	K	N	A	B	D
T	R	O	T	S	P	C	P	I	Q	Y	X	T	I	D
C	A	L	Y	Y	R	A	I	C	I	F	E	N	E	B
U	N	I	B	T	T	E	N	D	F	F	M	E	C	A
D	C	C	V	I	I	P	V	T	X	P	R	N	O	L
E	E	Y	O	C	M	L	R	I	E	H	E	A	L	L
D	T	N	W	O	E	K	I	E	N	E	T	M	L	E
P	A	H	T	L	A	E	H	B	M	U	D	R	I	R
L	S	Y	Y	T	I	L	I	B	A	I	L	E	S	B
H	O	M	E	O	W	N	E	R	S	S	U	P	I	M
R	E	N	E	W	A	B	L	E	L	O	I	M	O	U
C	O	V	E	R	A	G	E	V	R	D	Z	D	N	F

Make Your Vocation Your Vacation

Similar to the TV game show, Wheel of Fortune, fill in the blanks to reveal a message. Letters appear in random order, there is no "code."

A	B	C	D	E	F	G	H	I	J	K	L	M	N	O	P	Q	R	S	T	U	V	W	X	Y	Z
12	1	9	20	5	4	14		21		2	17	18	7	15	19		8	10	24	23	11			26	

L I F E   I S   N E V E R   M A D E
17 21 4 5   21 10   7 5 11 5 8   18 12 20 5

U N B E A R A B L E   B Y
23 7 1 5 12 8 12 1 17 5   1 26

C I R C U M S T A N C E S
9 21 8 9 23 18 10 24 12 7 9 5 10

B U T   O N L Y   B Y   L A C K   O F
1 23 24   15 7 17 26   1 26   17 12 9 2   15 4

M E A N I N G   A N D   P U R P O S E
18 5 12 7 21 7 14   12 7 20   19 23 8 19 15 10 5

No Collectors... No Problem!

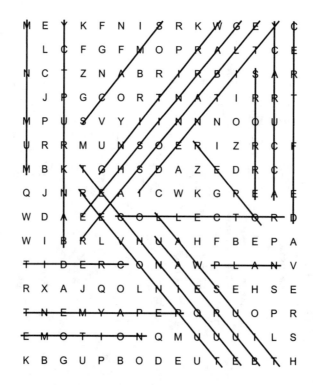

M	E	Y	K	F	N	I	S	R	K	W	G	E	Y	C
I	L	C	F	G	F	M	O	P	R	A	L	T	C	E
N	C	T	Z	N	A	B	R	I	R	B	I	S	A	R
I	J	P	G	C	O	R	T	N	A	T	I	R	R	T
M	P	U	S	V	Y	I	I	N	N	N	O	O	U	I
U	R	R	M	U	N	S	O	E	R	I	Z	R	C	F
M	B	K	T	G	H	S	D	A	Z	E	D	R	C	I
Q	J	N	R	E	A	I	C	W	K	G	R	E	A	E
W	D	A	E	E	C	O	L	L	E	C	T	O	R	D
W	I	B	R	L	V	H	U	A	H	F	B	E	P	A
T	I	D	E	R	C	O	N	A	W	P	L	A	N	V
R	X	A	J	Q	O	L	N	I	E	S	E	H	S	E
T	N	E	M	Y	A	P	E	R	Q	R	U	O	P	R
E	M	O	T	I	O	N	Q	M	U	U	U	I	L	S
K	B	G	U	P	B	O	D	E	U	T	E	B	T	H

One Last Thought: The Amazing Free Car Story

We normally buy:

An $18,000 new car at 10% payments of $300.00 a month - Value of car after 7 years is $800.00

Or why not try this???

Buy a $6000.00 used car for 7 years at 10% payments of $100.00 a month - Value of car after 7 years is $400.00.

Take the other $200.00 a month you would have paid above for the new car and save it for the same seven years at 10%, you will have $24,190.00 to pay cash for a car!

Who made the right choice??? Why not have "Free Cars" the rest of your life?

AT YEAR SEVEN:

The car is junk, in either plan after seven years, but in our plan:

Savings	$24,190.00
One Year Old Car for Cash	$16,000.00
Left in Savings	$ 8,190.00

NO CAR PAYMENTS!!!

ANOTHER SEVEN YEARS:

Save $300.00 per month from year 7 to year 14, plus interest in your savings of $8190.00 (10% return) the car is junk, again.

Savings	$52,245.00
One year old car for cash	$25,000.00
Left in savings	$27,245.00

NO CAR PAYMENTS!!!

You can continue to have "FREE CARS" the rest of your life because you puchased a lower priced car one time 14 years ago!!!